"Trauma has always been a part of the Asian American experience—for refugees, immigrants, and those living in the US for generations. Helen Hsu's work provides an important, culturally responsive approach that begins with an understanding of ourselves and our values, how we make wise decisions, and the importance of community."

> —**DJ Ida, PhD**, executive director of the National Asian American Pacific Islander
> Mental Health Association (NAAPIMHA)

"This is the workbook that clinicians and clients have been waiting for—a trauma-informed manual imbued with cultural humility that takes in the whole experience of Asian American trauma survivors—from the individual to the societal levels. Helen Hsu infuses her years of clinical experience with diverse Asian American communities throughout this book and its exercises."

> —**Ramani Durvasula, PhD**, clinical psychologist and author

"Helen Hsu has written a must-read resource that serves as a beacon of empowerment and healing for the Asian American community. Addressing the intersection of cultural identity and mental health, she offers invaluable tools for navigating trauma with sensitivity and understanding. Utilize this workbook—and learn from the best!"

> —**Christine Catipon, PsyD**, president of the Asian American
> Psychological Association (AAPA)

"*The Healing Trauma Workbook for Asian Americans* is a gift for Asian Americans interested in addressing the types of trauma that have been historically unaddressed for generations. Borrowing from traditional psychology and diverse Asian practices, Helen Hsu identifies root causes of traumatic stress and offers strategies toward healing. With examples inclusive of various ethnicities, generations, migration histories, and intersectional identities, this workbook is worthwhile reading for all Asian Americans."

> —**Kevin Nadal, PhD**, distinguished professor at City University of New York,
> president of the Filipino American National Historical Society, and author
> of *Microaggressions and Traumatic Stress*

"This is such an important topic! Helen Hsu has written the book we all need, whether we are clinicians/psychiatrists/psychologists or people struggling with trauma ourselves (or both). Hsu is both an academic and an experienced clinical psychologist helping people every day at Stanford. This workbook is practical and readable, but also well-referenced and evidence-based. Healing requires both the heart and the mind, and Hsu's book helps with both."

—**Rona J. Hu, MD**, clinical professor of psychiatry at Stanford University School of Medicine, founder of Stanford Mental Health for Asians Research and Treatment Clinic, and faculty of the Center for Asian Health Research and Education

"*The Healing Trauma Workbook for Asian Americans* speaks genuinely to the beautiful diversity of the Asian American community. Asian Americans navigate harms imposed by violence, microaggressions, stereotypes, and the hardships of migration and acculturation. In this workbook, every passage, activity, and reflection deepens connections to personal values, relationships, cultural wisdom, and the body/mind. It is a must-have for Asian Americans who wish to thrive in response to trauma."

—**Lou Felipe, PhD**, associate professor in the Graduate School of Professional Psychology at the University of Denver, and coeditor of *Clinical Interventions for Internalized Oppression*

The

Healing Trauma
Workbook *for*
Asian Americans

Heal from Racism, Build Resilience &
Find Strength in Your Identity

HELEN H. HSU, PSYD

New Harbinger Publications, Inc.

Publisher's Note

NEW HARBINGER PUBLICATIONS is a registered trademark of New Harbinger Publications, Inc.

New Harbinger Publications is an employee-owned company.

Copyright © 2024 by Helen H. Hsu

      New Harbinger Publications, Inc.

      5720 Shattuck Avenue

      Oakland, CA 94609

      www.newharbinger.com

Cover design by Sara Christian

Acquired by Elizabeth Hollis Hansen

Edited by Brady Kahn

Printed in the United States of America

26   25   24

10   9   8   7   6   5   4   3   2   1   First Printing

From my teachers to my students. Relative to relative. Elders to youth.

Contents

Foreword

I met psychologist Dr. Helen Hsu at the 2016 Asian American Psychological Association conference. I was the keynote speaker, and she was about to become the association's president.

I was uncomfortable.

Officially, I was an assistant professor at Columbia University Medical Center doing the serious work of helping people overcome their anxiety disorders. At the same time, I moonlit as a YouTuber, making goofy videos about the hidden psychology in science fiction films, video games, and comic books.

Those worlds didn't gel together well, at least in my head. And I was worried about being exposed as a contradiction in front of my elders, peers, and the next generation.

Dr. Hsu took me aside before my talk and expressed excitement about meeting me in person. She had been following my work for years at Columbia and on YouTube. "I love everything you said in your Psychology of Spock video! It helped me to see ethnic identity in a new way."

I can't tell you how much that put me at ease. To have this person I admire see these different parts of me and not judge them, just let them be, it was healing and gave me the confidence to give that talk.

Dr. Hsu just sees identity, time, and space differently. If you have the privilege of getting one-on-one support from her, you'll notice she simultaneously:

1. Stays with you in the present moment.

2. Evokes the total history of your ancestors.

3. Invites you to imagine your future as an elder in your community.

I don't know how she does this! It's all very timey wimey.

That's why she's the perfect person to write this book. Trauma is both about now and then. It isn't logical or linear. And for those of us who identify as Asian Americans, we need the integration of tradition along with the seemingly contradicting things that help us feel safe and seen right now.

Dr. Hsu understands that.

She practices that.

She's helped me to do that.

In the summer of 2020, I developed insomnia. I never had problems sleeping before, but now I couldn't stop thinking about the COVID-19 pandemic, what this meant for my daughter's future, and if I'd ever be able to see my elderly parents who lived halfway around the world again.

I reached out to Dr. Hsu for help (and recorded our conversation because that's what a YouTuber does). She taught me new ways to approach my bodymind, stuff I never considered before, like body scan meditations, muscle relaxation, and visualization. I experimented, and while not every skill worked for me, one did, and I could sleep again.

The same will likely be true for you. There are a lot of fantastic exercises inside this book. Not everything is going to work. You have to experiment and see what is most essential and effective for where you are in your life right now.

But rest assured, you are in good hands. Dr. Hsu understands trauma and respects the diversity of Asian American culture. She has helped so many who are in the exact position you are in right now.

I wish she could travel into the past instead of just evoking it. If she could give 15-year-old me a copy of this book, it would have saved me from years of unnecessary suffering.

Then again, she'd probably tell me, "You are who you are today because of the things you've experienced in the past, and who you are today doesn't have to be the person you become in the future."

Ali Mattu, PhD
Psychologist
San Francisco, CA

Introduction

Welcome to your journey of healing and resilience. It is my hope that our time together over these pages will provide useful tools for ongoing growth. The inspiration for this workbook emerged from my twenty years of experience as an educator and clinical psychologist with a therapy specialty supporting Asian Americans. I've had the honor of working with a wide range of Asian Americans of all ages: from Asian immigrants and refugees at community-based clinics to high-earning tech workers in my private practice, from youth and families in elementary and high schools to the elderly in geriatric services and hospice. I am currently a psychotherapist at Stanford University, where almost a quarter of the student body is composed of Asians and Asian Americans. Consistent across all these settings, one request has been constant: a desire for mental health and wellness self-help tools that respect, understand, and include Asian American life experiences and cultural values.

Western-trained counselors and authors have historically ignored or invalidated Asian American perspectives. The most famous and oft-quoted psychological theorists have all been from Western individualistic and industrialized countries. In fact, a recent article in the *American Psychologist* noted that 89 percent of the world's population is neglected in published English language psychology journals (Hall et al. 2021).

There are aspects of Western psychology that translate well into tools for other communities. Yet as Asian Americans, we seek healthy ways to understand and cope with complex experiences—intergenerational trauma, racial identity concerns, imposter phenomenon, and experiences of harassment and racism—through a cultural lens that includes communal obligations, saving face, and filial piety. Our heritage cultures have taught and practiced mind–body health activities such as meditation, yoga, and tai chi for literally thousands of years. We can reclaim this wisdom and integrate it with contemporary psychological science to address modern-day trauma recovery.

This workbook addresses recovery from traumatic experiences that are commonly experienced by Asian Americans. Studies of adverse childhood experiences (ACEs) demonstrate a strong correlation between past traumatic events and long-term health and well-being (Crandall et al. 2019). These experiences put you at a greater risk for negative health conditions. All people are vulnerable to traumas such as car accidents or natural disasters. Yet as Asian Americans we may carry added burdens of trauma. Some are systemic and familial, derived from intergenerational traumas including immigration, war or colonialism in our heritage countries, and chronic stressors such as the impacts of racism. These factors also play into our personal traumas, including being targeted for assault or harassment based upon our identities or suffering abuse or exploitation from traumatized or dysfunctional family and community members. One often hears boomers or Gen X adults complain about values and communication gaps with millennials and Gen Z young people—and vice versa. For Asian Americans, that generation gap is additionally complicated by layers of other differences in cultural and life experiences that can negatively impact coping and healing from traumatic experiences.

As you make your way through this workbook, embrace the richness of your individual journey. It's true that complexity can create challenges, yet I find that it can offer profound benefits and value. I have focused the book on Asian Americans because that is my own identity and the identity of those I most frequently have the privilege of working with. I hope that readers with other multilayered identities, such as Asian Australians and Asian Canadians, will also find useful content in these pages. Similarly, I hope that this book may be useful to some in our Asian Pacific Islander Desi American (APIDA) communities, but I do not want to claim ownership or expertise beyond my scope. In addition, many Asian Americans identify with BIPOC communities. You might have heard the acronym BIPOC, which refers to Black, indigenous, and people of color. I often use the term *people of the global majority* (PGM) to describe the values and experiences I share with a majority of cultures across the globe. This term intentionally corrects the more often used expression "minorities" to refer to Asian Americans and other people of color. We are not a minority. In fact, Asians are a clear global majority, as the most populous countries are China and India. At any rate, you can see how Asian Americans may share many topics of interest with other communities, and I recommend readings and resources at the end of this workbook highlighting experts from communities I cannot represent.

Being a person with a multifaceted identity and experience does sometimes come with unique stressors. Yet along with the stress, Asian Americans also develop unique strengths. The history of Asian Americans is full of examples and stories of resilience, loyalty, and ingenuity. There's enormous value in what narrative therapists refer to as "thickening" our stories. This refers to creating a narrative, a mental storytelling and understanding of ourselves, that encompasses our full complexity. You are much too interesting to be living within narrow black-and-white definitions and one-dimensional expectations. Let us create and live within what Pulitzer prize-winning author Viet Thanh Nguyen refers to as "narrative plentitude."

I've heard Asian Americans tell me they feel unseen, invisible, or fragmented in their communities. Many of us have had experiences of being pressured into masking our true selves or feeling shamed for being complex and different. Many of us have experienced microaggressions, racism, and trauma targeting our identities as part of a nondominant culture. Let's explore ways you can heal and feel seen, acknowledged, and whole. I hope you use this workbook as a step to proactively protect your holistic health and overall well-being.

Many in the Asian American community feel uncomfortable seeking professional counseling or lack the financial resources to do so. There are also numerous cities where it feels impossible to find an Asian American therapist or any therapist well-trained in cultural humility and culturally sensitive mental health care. The vulnerable work of therapy can be hampered when working with a therapist who does not comprehend or value Asian American experiences.

This workbook is a resource tailored to help you heal from traumas you may have experienced as an Asian American, and to support and enrich your emotional health and mind–body resilience. The information in this book cites well-researched psychological studies and introduces therapy self-help skills. The exercises will help you shed harmful mindsets imposed by dysfunctional systems. Together, the readings and workbook exercises are a guide to learn and rehearse practical skills.

This workbook will guide you to

- Cultivate positive racial identity

- Clarify values

- Develop mind–body health practices

- Reduce unhelpful thinking habits

- Modulate emotional ups and downs

- Manage stressors

- Recover from setbacks

- Improve relationships and community connection

Each chapter focuses on a different facet of Asian American mental health to help you strengthen these facets of yourself:

- Identity

- Values

- Mind–body health

- Reasoning

- Emotional modulation

- Healing

- Relationships and community

- Empowerment

These components of Asian American mental health support emotional resilience.

How to Use This Workbook

Each chapter will introduce data and research findings, community examples, and guided activities for your personal reflection, growth, and practice. Some free tools are also available at http://www.newharbinger.com/52724. Making time to learn ultimately decreases anxiety. When we understand the processes and reasons for our own and others' behaviors, our experience can feel less overwhelming or confusing. Learning helps us see the ways we are not alone in even our most embarrassing and painful feelings. It can also provide us with tools to maximize coping.

Personal reflection is also key to overcoming trauma. The worst thing to do when we are stressed is to overthink. All too often, internal worrying can lead us into a loop of negative rumination inside our heads. Reflection is a way to mentally take a step back and gain perspective. Self-reflection is an important activity to allow for honest self-assessment. This is foundational to understanding where you should focus your efforts.

Completing the recommended prompts and activities in the workbook is a form of practice. Have you ever sat awake at night and ruminated about what you wish you had said or done differently? Most of us know that feeling all too well. Practicing new thought and communication habits takes time. Having a chance to brainstorm or rehearse on paper helps you try out new ways of thinking and responding.

Research shows that when we journal, create art, draw, talk, sing, or diagram, it can be a game changer in terms of understanding ourselves and the situation at hand. These practices help us gain clarity and perspective. Changing our modality of processing can tap into self-awareness, activate different brain regions, and allow us to consider new ways of thinking and coping.

Sometimes it's going to be uncomfortable. For example, a reading section might bring up a memory that triggers an upsetting emotion or physical feeling. Please understand that discomfort doesn't mean you are doing things wrong! As with physical exercise, a moderate amount of discomfort is a normal part of building strength. What it does mean is that you might benefit from using a coping skill or grounding skill before continuing. It could mean that this is a good time to take a break to stretch, or it could mean this is a topic to explore further by talking with a trusted friend, advisor, or counselor.

At the end of each chapter, you will review the main ideas and points. Take some time to note ideas for how to maintain new skills. Ask yourself, what are the main takeaways that you can apply in your life? Think about goals for continued learning. Be patient and curious with the process. For example, it took a lot of intentional practice for me to change the negative, problematic thoughts I had rehearsed for years during my formative teen years. I had to learn and recite more balanced, accurate, and healthy ways of thinking. It initially felt awkward. I had setbacks when I would slide into old habits of negative thinking. It took months of rehearsing alternative, more balanced thoughts before they started to replace my outdated mental scripts.

This workbook is an introductory guide for part of your journey to wholeness, health, and posttraumatic growth. At the end, you'll find a list of other resources to explore as you continue to heal and grow. It is possible to thrive and flourish as a survivor of trauma, and this workbook will discuss many examples of skills that other Asian Americans have used in their healing journeys.

I was raised in a cultural environment that never talked about mental health, and where stoic endurance of suffering was seen as admirable. If this is also true for you, let your first cognitive reframe, your first shift in thinking, be this: *Seeking mental health support is not a sign of weakness.*

Seeking mental health support and proactively exploring new skills is smart, empowering, and generous. There is no need to do things the hard way when tools and experts can ease the endeavor. It is empowering to make authentic choices for yourself. It is generous to put forth efforts that can bring generational healing into your heart, your family, and your community. We deserve to heal from trauma, and to resist further harm from oppressive and hurtful narratives and systems. Seeking justice and healing takes place at every level, in your individual struggle, your family story, in community growth, and in activism for ancestors and future generations. I thank you for being a part of the Asian American community that is breaking down mental health stigma and utilizing wisdom about holistic health.

Chapter 1

How You Define Yourself

Decades of psychological research have demonstrated a correlation between positive racial or ethnic identity and protective mental health factors. This means that when you feel positive about your racial and ethnic identity, your mental health is more resilient. So how do you develop a positive sense of identity? It's the kind of goal that sounds far simpler than it is. All our lives our families push for us to identify in particular ways, yet we're also exposed to cultural, community, and historical factors that influence identity in other ways. It's not a matter of choosing a right or a correct identity. The identities promoted and taught by others may not always be ones that resonate and feel authentic for you. You may be different, and different does not mean bad or good. For example, my grandmother had a strong positive ethnic and cultural identity as Chinese. She felt strongly connected to the Chinese community. My identity is different and more complicated. I also feel a strong and positive ethnic and cultural identity, but as an Asian American immigrant from Taiwan, of Chinese and Mongolian heritage. I feel strong bonds with multiple racial and ethnic communities.

You might feel grounded and proud of your identity, or you may feel like you don't know where you fit in. A fundamental point: nobody else gets to define who you are. Asian America includes people who may be recent immigrants, 1.5 generation folks, "third culture kids," transracial adoptees, of fourth or fifth generations, and Asians of multiple or mixed heritage. Asian America includes people who are LGBTQIA+, neurodiverse, have various spiritual beliefs, are disabled, or may speak English or multiple other languages at home. We are a bimodal demographic, which means Asian Americans occupy both the very highest and very lowest levels of educational and economic security in the whole country. We are from every caste and have various economic, religious, and political affiliations. Your identity contains multiple intersecting realities. Nobody has a monopoly on what defines Asian America, although plenty of people will try to put their opinions or stereotypes upon you.

Asian Americans are a unique group of communities with lots of intergroup diversity. Asian Americans come from forty-eight different ethnic groups with unique histories of immigration, citizenship, and experiences, yet we are often lumped together and stereotyped. This can even come from within our own families.

Holding two or more identities is complicated. It can be tiring to experience the assumptions and interpretations of others who don't really know you yet impose their perspective. There are advantages to blending and knowing more than one culture, but it can be hard to understand your identity when you don't feel seen or understood, and this is particularly hard in your youth or at important life stages. Most Asian Americans who reside in North American have experienced being actively invalidated or ridiculed by microaggressions or seeing media representations of racist stereotypes. Those of us who are Gen X grew up with degrading depictions of Asian American characters in film and on television being mocked, vilified, or exploited. Often Asian Americans experience racism based upon inaccurate stereotypes, or from people making fun of food, language, or customs they don't understand. These types of experiences contribute to problems developing a positive sense of Asian American identity. In addition, racial stereotypes contribute to traumatizing experiences such as bullying and assault.

Professors Frank Chin and Jeffery Paul Chan (1972) described the model minority stereotype as "racist love"—supposedly good to be seen as a "model minority" but in fact emasculating and paternalistic. The model minority myth has been used to cause divisions between Asian American and Black and Brown communities and to paint Asians in a very narrow manner. The model minority myth also contributes to the "bamboo ceiling," where successful and competent Asian Americans find their career growth limited as a result of the stereotype that Asians are hard workers but supposedly lack leadership and innovation skills (Shao 2023). Author Prachi Gupta's memoir (2023) articulates how colonialism and the model minority myth directly harms Asian American families like her own.

Let's look at some examples.

Phil was born and grew up in San Francisco. *His relatives would tease and make fun of him as "not Chinese" or a "banana" because he wasn't fluent in Cantonese and had never visited Hong Kong. Now a college student in Ohio, he's frustrated when professors or peers assume he's a foreigner or a math major just because he looks Asian. He's most comfortable with the diverse friends of his intramural soccer team, but his parents warn him not to trust non-Chinese people. He worries about his parents being victimized in an anti-Asian hate crime. Phil sometimes feels like he's not fully at home anywhere.*

Lena is a Korean American adoptee. *Her white family members deny they "see" her race. She knows her family loves her, but it hurts that no one understands her whole self. Her family states she is "one of them" and won't acknowledge the confusing and sometimes lonely experiences she has had as a transracial adoptee. She also feels unsure if she is "Asian enough" to be welcomed into the Asian American Employee Resource Group at her workplace.*

Sophy is a Cambodian American born in Arizona. *Her parents don't talk about their family history, because it reminds them of painful memories. Sophy wishes she knew more about her culture and her parents' hometown. All she knows is that several family members were killed in war. It was traumatic for her parents, and they lived in a refugee camp a couple years before* *they got sponsored to come to the United States. She doesn't like it when people just assume she is Chinese or Filipino, and she's also bothered by sexism within her community. She feels distant and unsure what it means to be a Cambodian American woman. She didn't have any Cambodian American role models at school, and she doesn't see any in the media either.*

Self-Reflection

Reflect on the questions and respond in the space provided:

Have you ever experienced a situation where you were made to feel as if you were not "Asian enough" or just not what was expected from an Asian?

_____

_____

_____

_____

_____

Have you ever experienced a situation where you were made to feel as if you were "too Asian" or just not "American enough?"

_____

_____

_____

_____

_____

Can you recall a situation or time where you felt completely accepted and at ease with your sense of self and identity? Describe the aspects which helped you feel that way.

_____

_____

_____

_____

_____

_____

_____

_____

Encountering Stereotypes

Stereotypes are gross overgeneralizations about a group of people, such as Asian Americans. It's true that all humans tend to use broad mental schemas to understand the world. Yet stereotypes are not simply overgeneralized misunderstandings. In the context of world history and oppression, stereotypes have been used as a tool to justify oppression or exclusion. Colonial powers including Spain, England, and the United States have promoted propaganda about Asian countries as being inferior to Western or European countries to justify the "need" for invasions. White men in the United States have spread demasculinizing and negative stereotypes about Asian men in response to feeling threatened about competing with Asian labor. Historical wartime exploitation of Asian women has contributed to harmful sexualized or servitude-oriented stereotypes. Stereotyping Asian Americans, whether as perpetual foreigners or as a model minority, is a dehumanizing generalization that obscures the unique qualities and traits of each Asian American person.

Here are some common stereotypes of Asian Americans. Have you experienced anyone making assumptions about you based on these stereotypes? Check off any that you've encountered:

☐ Foreigner

☐ Fresh off the boat (FOB)

☐ Hard working

☐ Math whiz

☐ Can't speak English

☐ Service worker

☐ Sexualized

☐ Desexualized

☐ Exotic

☐ Submissive or passive

☐ Sneaky

☐ Dirty

☐ Disease carrying

☐ Eating "weird' things

☐ Model minority

☐ Obedient

☐ Crazy rich/privileged

☐ Poor

Examine Stereotype Sources

What are some of the stereotypes you have heard of or experienced within your own family?

_____

_____

_____

_____

_____

_____

_____

What are some of the stereotypes you have heard of or experienced from media or culture outside your home?

_____

_____

_____

_____

_____

_____

_____

As you write down these stereotypes, take a moment to examine them. Do these labels feel degrading? Funny? Empowering? Confusing? Where do you think the assumptions came from?

_____

_____

_____

_____

_____

_____

_____

San Francisco Bay Area poet, educator, and community organizer Terisa Siagatonu (2023) shares a commitment to the notion that writing and telling our own stories is essential for well-being and health. As we live within a dominant narrative, a certain story or explanation that supports dominant social group interests exists. It is maintained by repetition, told by those with authority, and by silencing other narratives. Speaking your truth destabilizes dominant narratives which may be unhealthy for you. Cultural change always comes before political or social change.

Shifting the Narrative

Recently, you may have heard about some schools adding Asian American history to the required curriculum. Research demonstrates that ethnic studies can help all students by promoting compassion and understanding, building critical-thinking skills in understanding racism and race relations, and increasing student involvement in civic engagement and advocacy (Sleeter and Zavala 2020). This curriculum can help us combat systemic stereotypes about Asian Americans and other groups.

Our families also carry narratives, and these contain both helpful and unhelpful stories. Many of our families operated in "survival mode," employing strategies and behaviors to survive without having the opportunity to critically examine identity and sense of self. We continue to evolve from our old stories as we encounter different terrain, new situations, new life experiences, and demands. For example, what we explore in therapy are the ways that old stories and habits, which may have made sense in our family of origin or hometown, may now be outdated, unhelpful, or overly simplified. The old ways may not have been wrong in their time and place, but they might get us stuck and lack usefulness for us now.

Let's look at some examples of Asian Americans learning to shift their internal story narratives.

Winnie used to feel imposter syndrome. *She felt had to prove she deserved to be at her college or workplace. As a kid, she was embarrassed by the accent in her parents' spoken English. Her parents taught her to "be quiet and work hard." She felt like she had to overcompensate, and she overworked at the office to prove her value. After reading books about Chinese American history, Winnie began to develop a growing sense of pride and belonging, she says. "I didn't know that Chinese Americans played such a major role in building this region, this country, and that our roots go back to the 1800s." She has begun to speak up more in meetings and is getting comfortable with taking up space, being firm about getting credit for her work. Winnie is realizing that a lot of her worries about being not good enough were in her own mind, and not* *how her coworkers saw her. She also understands that while staying quiet was her parents' way of feeling safe, for Winnie, speaking up is what creates safety and stability.*

Manny's family always played favorites with his younger brother Len, who has fair skin. *They'd comment that Len was more handsome than other family members and that he would be more successful than Manny. Manny states, "It used to give me such a complex and, of course, hurt my feelings. My Filipino American professor taught me what colonial mentality and internalized oppression is, which helped me realize the internal racism in how my family acts. I found friends who celebrate our culture and #MagandangMorenx [beautiful brown skin]. This helped me value myself. It's still annoying when family makes comments full of colorism, but I don't internalize it anymore. I feel sorry for them. Their comments are not about me and my worth, but reveal a lot of their own insecurities and bad experiences."*

Self-Reflection

What are some factors that have shaped how you see and define yourself?

- ☐ Parents
- ☐ Elders
- ☐ Siblings
- ☐ Extended family
- ☐ Celebrities
- ☐ Magazines/books/comics
- ☐ Television shows
- ☐ Movies
- ☐ Games

- ☐ Social media
- ☐ Classmates
- ☐ Teachers
- ☐ Employers
- ☐ Dating partners
- ☐ Friends
- ☐ Neighborhood
- ☐ Spiritual leader or community

Examining Your Narrative

Think about the messages you have picked up from different sources. Have these messages been helpful? Harmful? Sometimes mixed? What systems or people benefit from perpetuating internalized oppressions or negative stereotypes of Asian Americans? Practice asking these questions periodically as you take intentional control in defining the narratives of your identity. Are there some sources you would like to leave behind? Are there others you would like to seek out?

Winnie realized she would like to learn more about historical contributions of Chinese Americans. She deprioritized mainstream media, which never represented her experience, and started attending Center for Asian American Media (CAAM) events. She enjoys watching films that center on Asian American stories and creators.

Manny decided to watch more shows that feature Filipino American entertainers. He also began practicing mindfulness and perspective-taking skills to lessen the emotional impact of family elders saying hurtful things. He volunteers as a coach for his nephews' basketball team and strives to be a "positive Brown role model" to diverse youth.

Both Winnie and Manny have intentionally sought out friends and community where they feel valued and accepted as their whole selves.

Develop Your Own Narrative

Are there narratives or stories you would like to leave behind?

_____

_____

_____

_____

_____

_____

_____

What are the narratives or stories you would like to strengthen?

_____

_____

_____

_____

_____

What are the ways you define yourself? Identify places or people who help you feel the most at ease and whole (when you are in these places or with these people, you do not feel pressure to mask or fake a persona).

_____

_____

_____

_____

_____

Identify some aspects of your identity that feel most important to your authentic well-being.

_____

_____

_____

_____

_____

As you read over these thoughts, perhaps you will notice which places or people can be most helpful or harmful in your journey to build up a positive racial and cultural identity.

Let's take another look at Sophy's story as a source of inspiration. As you may recall, Sophy didn't learn much about her family's history growing up and felt unsure about what it meant to be a Cambodian American woman. Today Sophy is writing an honors thesis at university about the resilience of Cambodian genocide survivors. She plans to attend more Cambodian American cultural events and to speak up when people overlook or exclude Southeast Asian Americans from Asian American Pacific Islander (AAPI) spaces. She is expanding her interactions with extended family and seeking the stories of Cambodian American women, whose stories have not historically been well-preserved. Through social media, Sophy was thrilled to learn about several former refugee Aunties who had become successful small business owners. Sophy wants to leave behind the "victim" and "foreigner" identities in her family history and embrace the survivor and reinvention aspects of their stories. She reflects, "I grew up being told that being Cambodian was why we had problems. I've learned now that the problems came from war, politics, and racial systems of abusive power. The values and connections my family has been able to preserve are a testament to our strong resilience."

Attuning to Yourself

Take note when something does not feel right in your interactions. This could be a microaggression or overt racism or other bias. As we move through this workbook, you will hone your awareness and instinct. Awareness is the first step in learning how to distance yourself from stereotypes, people, and situations that do not validate your whole presence and identity. This may seem like merely a symbolic or semantic matter, but part of the harm trauma causes is that it damages our trust in ourselves and sense of mindful presence. Every small step in reclaiming self-definition is part of healing.

As Asian Americans, we are Americans who have ancestry from ancient cultures across the world. As Asians, we are part of the people of the global majority (PGM). As Americans, we hold roles and identities in our current communities. Write down the aspects of how you define yourself.

Who you are: _____

_____

_____

_____

_____

Who you are not: _____

_____

_____

_____

_____

Your sense of identity can change quite a bit over your lifetime. One model that may help you think about identity development is the Racial and Cultural Identity Development Model (Sue and Sue 1990). This model outlines five stages:

Stage 1: Conformity. Unquestioning support for values of dominant culture.

Stage 2: Dissonance. Life experience challenges your self-concept, leading you to question previously held beliefs and identification with dominant culture.

Stage 3: Resistance and immersion. Complete rejection of values of the dominant culture. You replace these values with minority-held views. Sense of shame or guilt that in accepting values of the dominant culture, you were betraying your own cultural group and supporting social oppression.

Stage 4: Introspection. Period of questioning group views as being too rigid or in conflict with your own views.

Stage 5. Integrative awareness. Recognition that all cultures have both acceptable and unacceptable aspects and that we each must determine what makes sense for ourselves.

Where do you feel you presently are in the racial identity model? What stage feels most safe, comfortable, and empowering for you?

_____

_____

_____

_____

_____

_____

_____

In this model you can see that the most developed identity stage is "integrative awareness." I quite like this term, as so much about our emotional health does rely on moving through discomfort and denial to reach a place of being present and integrated. When we experience trauma, we often survive by cutting off parts of ourselves. To cope with the distress of the trauma, we instinctively disassociate, deny, or avoid the experience. Others around us may invalidate, minimize, or justify the trauma, which further cuts us off from being integrated and whole. Similarly, we Asian Americans often hide or modify aspects of ourselves in efforts to gain approval from majority populations, again at the risk of losing our authentic selves. You do not have to exist fragmented or cut off from your whole, holistic self.

Here are three things you can do to continue to develop a strong positive racial ethnic intersectional identity. First, plan for ongoing learning. Reading through this book is a step in this direction. You don't have to clearly know in advance what your exact goals are, and some of your salient identities might not even be clear yet (for example, your sexual orientation, religious affiliation or disability status might change over your lifetime). Be intentional about seeking constructive identity influences and learning. Now is the time to practice curiosity and explore perspectives.

Lifelong learning can be as simple as setting tiny habits that regularly expose you to things that are affirming or new. Review your workbook responses throughout this journey and make note of key themes to strengthen and skills to practice.

Second, learn to detect and push away stories that try to make you small. Notice who and what impacts your identity story and feelings. You have the right to define and redefine your identity as life circumstances change and you evolve. For example, many older generation Asian Americans were accustomed to being referred to as "Oriental," but current generations of Asian Americans reject that term as an inaccurate racial slur. Or, as a child you may have embraced the model minority myth but as an adult you see yourself as a nuanced person defined by other things. In yet another example, I have worked with Asian Americans raised in unwelcoming communities who were told to "feel grateful" just for being allowed to participate. As they reclaimed their sense of worth, they shifted from feeling grateful, or like imposters, to feeling worthy, resilient, and confident.

The third thing you can do to develop your identity is to actively engage in your chosen communities. Feelings of belonging are crucial for mental health to flourish. In stressful times, especially, our bonds with others are mutually protective. Connection with others is protective of our health during the most stressful life experiences. Your presence, stories, and actions are also vital parts of community well-being. Chapter 7 will go into greater depth about the importance of community care and belonging.

Chapter 2

Root Yourself
in Values

As we go about our daily lives, rarely do we take the time to analyze the importance of our values. Why do values matter? Your values form the foundation of who you are. They guide your actions and choices, and determine what matters most in your life. Your values define what standards of behavior are acceptable or important to you. Though individuals, families, religions, cultures, and organizations may share some values, each person's core values are unique to them. This chapter will help you clarify the values you hold, to make you stronger and more rooted in who you are and what is most important to you.

Asian Americans are often poorly served by Eurocentric mental health guides, because these guides do not account for or recognize cultural differences in values. The most frequent criticism of Western therapy by Asian Americans is that Western approaches are excessively individualistic, which does not fit with common Asian values. In the United States, individual independence is a value of upmost importance, whereas for Asian cultures independence generally ranks far below other values such as preserving harmony, filial piety, humility, stoicism, achievement, and saving face. There is no universal scale to measure which values are better, as there are many different values and they are all important. The goal here is to identify and practice the distinct blend of values that defines and guides you. As an Asian American, this task is made complicated by the often contradictory messages you receive within a multicultural, multigenerational context.

Living your values offers a means to increase contentment, motivation, and belonging. Values provide a guide for making positive life choices. People who spend their time in ways that are supportive and congruent with their values feel happier and more satisfied than those whose lives don't reflect their values. Some stress or problems are inevitable in every life, yet you can attain contentment when you live in sync with your core values. Although things may not be perfect, you will experience satisfaction and some sense of internal peace from living in a way that is worthy and "good enough."

You know the saying "Do work you love and you will never work a day in your life"? This idea can be extended to living by your values. When we feel great about the value of what we are doing, it is much easier to stay interested and motivated to complete difficult tasks. For example, if you value education, you likely located in yourself the drive to take classes and complete assignments even when doing so felt grueling. You may have labored at jobs you didn't love but did so to provide stability and resources to your family or to save for something important. We persevere when we feel the task at hand is valuable.

Values also guide you to find people and places with shared ideals and interests. A sense of belonging is protective of mental health. Loneliness is correlated with negative physical and mental health consequences, including high blood pressure, cognitive decline, a weakened immune system, and anxiety. Shared values are fundamental for social connection and creating healthy relationships that contribute to your health and happiness. Good relationships are often created in spaces where people engage in activities that support shared values. If you value environmental causes, you are likely to feel a sense of belonging among other people who feel similarly. Likewise, you may have made friendships at your temple or church or while doing volunteer work, because these are places you can find others who share your values.

Ultimately, grounding yourself in core values creates a path to guide your life choices in a way that is true to your deepest self. Part of healing from trauma is unlearning survival habits or negative reactions that came from what has hurt you, and knowing your deepest values will help you create habits for healthy healing and growth. Your values provide a measure for you to use when making decisions and can help you avoid repeating unhealthy choices from the past.

In addition to the harm traumatic events may cause to your body, the painful incongruence between what you are told about the world and what you experience can have a significant damaging effect. The deep rift of traumatic events can contribute to a long-lasting sense of mistrust, confusion, and ongoing anxiety. You may feel this indirectly, as a crisis of faith when your belief in a just, fair world is proven wrong; or worse, you may have been targeted by actively manipulative behaviors, where someone denies your lived experiences and emotions through gaslighting.

Here are some examples of folks seeking to clarify their core values.

Thanh is a top technical sales representative. *He's known for charming clients, flashing his expensive watch, and treating everyone to rounds of cocktails or golf outings. Last season he had a horrible mountain biking accident. Thanh spent eleven days hospitalized, suffering broken bones and intense pain. He also felt mentally stunned, realizing that he had nearly died. The buddies he drank with weekly and the women he dated didn't visit him at the hospital. Thanh had always felt emotionally distant from his parents, as they never verbalized emotional support, yet they were a consistent care-taking presence throughout the hospitalization and eight weeks of grueling physical rehabilitation. Thanh was humbled and touched by his parents' dedication. He wants to be a supportive, reliable person of integrity too. Status symbols and excitement feel way less important to him now than they did before the accident. Thanh feels in his gut that to really recover from this accident will require more than just physical work. He is feeling a drive to create a more rewarding, values-grounded lifestyle.*

Jae works hard and was the first in their family to attend college in the US. *Jae's parents gave up white collar office jobs in Manila to toil long restaurant hours after immigrating. It was traumatizing to experience racist bullying in their new neighborhood. Jae feels a heavy sense of guilt and obligation. Jae is now in the final semester at college, preparing for job interviews. The career counselor asked what their values were in creating a life plan. Jae realized the family has been on survival mode for so long that they had never thought about values before. There were so many factors to think about. How should Jae rank the importance of living close to home? Salary? Purpose? Safety? Personal meaning? Every family member gave Jae conflicting advice about what was most important.*

Ryan is the youngest of five siblings in a Korean American pastor's family. *He feels ashamed of his family's secrets. He cannot reconcile the stated values of his family—charity, love, and compassion—with the physical abuse and relentless verbal cruelties in the family's home life. Ryan feels confused and angry about the hypocrisy. He is terrified of his own temper as he struggles with moodiness, anxiety, and "angry outbursts." When Ryan and his wife decided to start a family of their own, he chose to begin therapy. Therapy was the first place he allowed himself to talk about painful, humiliating things from his family history. He is building an action plan to uphold and practice values in his role as a new parent. Ryan still values charity, love, and compassion. He is being intentional about learning how to apply and live these values better than his own parents were able to.*

LeAnn is a survivor of childhood sexual abuse who feels lingering trauma. *Her abuser was an authority figure from school. He manipulated her loyalties and blamed her for his own reprehensible actions. With the support of her parents, therapist, and friends, LeAnn is unravelling the distortions and lies of her abuser. Clarifying her values with intention is helping her to push shame outward rather than internalize it. She is reading about sexual assault survivor and civil rights activist Amanda Nguyen and feels inspired to advocate for justice for other survivors as well.*

Identify Your Core Values

Think about what you find meaningful. What comes to mind? It can include activities, ideas, works of art, or places that inspire you. As an example, Thanh remembers feeling really moved when he heard an interview with the author Ocean Vuong speaking about resilience and family, and he remembers a deep sense of satisfaction alongside his uncle when his uncle taught him how to remodel a house. Write about anything you find meaningful.

_____

_____

_____

_____

_____

_____

We often feel fulfilled and completely present when we are engaged in something aligned with our values. Think about a time when you felt absorbed and in the moment. Who was with you and what were you doing? Ryan remembers feeling completely present and engaged when he volunteered as a tutor for children in an economically marginalized part of town. It was one of the rare times his anxiety went away and he felt incredibly patient. Write down your memories of a time when you were present and engaged in the moment.

_____

_____

_____

_____

_____

_____

What kinds of people do you find inspiring and worthy of admiration? Think of some local, worthy actions taken by people you know and not just the accomplishments of famous people. For example, Jae wrote that they admired not only wealthy entrepreneurs and Pope John Paul but also their family matriarch, Lola, for her great cooking and for being a tough and wise role model for the whole family. List at least five people.

_____

_____

_____

_____

_____

_____

_____

_____

_____

_____

_____

Reflect on your answers to the previous questions. Then read through the following list of values and circle those that are important to you. Do not overthink this. If none of these words match your values, you can also add different words at the end of the list. You may want to include words that are not in English. For example, Dr. Kevin Nadal (2012) writes about Filipino values of *kapwa* (connectedness), *pakikisama* (harmony), and *hiya* (honor.) If you are Buddhist, you might add values such as *mettā* (good will), *maitrī* (loving-kindness) or *upekkhā* (equanimity).

Achievement	Adventure	Authenticity
Authority	Autonomy	Balance
Beauty	Boldness	Citizenship
Community	Compassion	Competition
Connection	Contribution	Courage
Creativity	Equity	Excitement
Fame	Family	Filial Piety
Financial Security	Freedom	Fun
Generosity	Giving Back	Graciousness
Happiness	Harmony	Honesty
Independence	Influence	Integrity
Interdependence	Joy	Justice
Kindness	Learning	Legacy
Liberty	Love	Loyalty
Maturity	Mercy	Optimism
Originality	Peace	Personal Growth
Physical Well-Being	Pride	Respect
Responsibility	Safety	Self-Expression
Service	Spirituality	Status
Stoicism	Teamwork	Thrift
Tradition	Trustworthiness	Understanding
Uniqueness	Usefulness	Valor
Wealth	Wisdom	Other:
Other:	Other:	Other:
Other:	Other:	Other:

Now, put stars by the most important values you circled. Choose as many as eight. Pick what feels right in your gut, not what you think you "should" pick. Jot some notes down about why these values stand out for you.

_____

_____

_____

_____

_____

_____

_____

_____

_____

_____

_____

Next, consider what your top three values would be. Rank and prioritize how important these values are in your life.

Value 1: _____

Value 2: _____

Value 3: _____

Pause now to take a deep, cleansing breath.

Clarify Your Values

Review your top three values with a spirit of curiosity. Where did these values come from? Sometimes we inherit our values from our family or community members, who may have explicitly shared these values. Other times we figure out our values on our own or through what we have observed. Sometimes we may simply feel a value as deeply resonant within our hearts, even if others do not share the same opinion. For example, Thanh noticed that values about achievement and accomplishment have stemmed from his desire to impress others, and his greater current motivation to live with integrity and be a supportive person feels more aligned with values that are personally meaningful. Identify and write down the sources for your top three values.

Source 1: _____

Source 2: _____

Source 3: _____

Now being honest—setting aside judgment—ask yourself which of these values personally resonate deeply in your heart and gut. Are there other values that feel more like "shoulds," or seem heavy with obligations to others? For example, LeAnn wrote down "motherhood" as a value and also notices that she feels intense pressure from her community to make motherhood her primary life goal. She does want to start a family someday, but decided not to include "motherhood" among her top three values, because currently she would rather take a different path to grow as a person. She still struggles with feeling like something must be wrong with her current values, because others would choose differently. Look at all the values you circled and write down the ones you feel you "ought to" care about and if you feel obligated to others rather than yourself.

_____

_____

_____

_____

The purpose of this clarification is not to shame or judge, but simply to step back and observe, notice, and identify. The goal is greater self-awareness. Perhaps you notice that you have three top values, but that one of them is influenced more by pressures from society than by what feels authentic and true for you. That's normal. Accepting and living with complications is part of learning to be whole. Writing down your thoughts is a step toward finding your own ways to uphold and practice your cultural values.

It's also important to clarify if you interpret an important value differently than others do. For example, Ryan's father accused him of betraying family loyalty. His father defined "family loyalty" as obedience and keeping his father's secrets, but to Ryan family loyalty means protecting his family from further harm, which entails dismantling abusive traits and facing truths. His greatest hope is that traumatic intergenerational patterns of abuse will end. Take a moment to think about any disagreements or differing views you have experienced about how to apply your values. Write down how you see certain values differently from others.

_____

_____

_____

_____

_____

_____

_____

_____

_____

_____

Consider how you may acknowledge others' opinions and choose a different way to practice an important value for you. For example, Jae noticed that living in the same town as their family felt like an expectation and obligation. They treasure family values but felt that they could maintain closeness even if they moved to a new town to pursue career growth. Write about any value you are aware of that you want to keep on your own terms.

_____

_____

_____

_____

_____

_____

_____

_____

_____

_____

We do not live in an ideal world. Sometimes we must make compromises for the sake of survival and our safety when navigating systems of power. Living your values is not an all-or-nothing endeavor. I want you to be strategic and care for yourself in this process. In *The Ethical Sell Out*, authors Lily Zheng and Inge Hansen (2019) delve into different ways to address ethical dilemmas in a world that requires compromise. This might look like waiting to be as fully outspoken as you would like to be until you have earned more power in your career, and then leveraging your privileged position to speak up for newer or younger employees. It could be compromising temporarily on your value of authenticity because you live in an unsafe environment where people react irrationally to truth. It is okay to keep your goals modest and manageable for your current life stage.

As you strive to live your values, don't forget to include yourself! It is common for Asian Americans and other people with collectivistic values to neglect themselves or hold different standards for self and others. Think about the Buddhist value of loving-kindness: it is a practice of radical love for all and includes learning to speak to yourself with kindness and compassion as well. This might be an unfamiliar practice. For example, LeAnn consistently extended grace and forgiveness to others but was harsh and shaming in her self-talk.

Practice Your Values

Can you think of some ways to practice small, everyday activities that align with your core values? For example, Thanh identified three very simple actions that feel good and align with his values: to call and check in on his parents more often; to be more generous when tipping service workers; and to give praise and credit to colleagues at work and likewise accept recognition for himself. As you can see, your goals do not have to involve massive changes. Write down some everyday actions that can bring you closer to living your values.

_____

_____

_____

_____

_____

_____

_____

_____

Are you able to think of ways to consistently include your own wellness as valuable? LeAnn decided to practice reciting a brief guided meditation for self-compassion each morning as well as to engage in little acts of generosity like baking pastries for friends and helping her grand-mother run errands. The self-compassion meditation helped her feel calmer and also fueled her ability to feel more generous and present for others. Write down some ways to support your own wellness. Again, these can be modest actions, not necessarily dramatic or big in scale.

_____

_____

_____

_____

_____

_____

_____

_____

_____

Ultimately, knowing your values allows you to develop a life plan that is interwoven with your values. Now that you have identified some everyday practices, you can plan how to apply them consistently. It takes a lot of practice for a new habit to become a comfortable routine. Progress happens over time. Often new habits fail when people try to take on drastic changes at an unrea-sonable pace. For example, smoking cessation or daily exercise are common New Year's resolu-tions. Yet to change from daily smoking to zero smoking is unlikely for most people. Likewise, to jump from zero exercise to daily exercise would be exceedingly difficult. Small, specific steps toward goals are more likely to succeed than big, grand efforts that may quickly run out of steam.

You've already started taking small and specific actions to practice your values. Now, looking back at your list of top three values, can you think of some additional actions that you would be interested in practicing in the future?

_____

_____

_____

_____

_____

_____

_____

You can make these practices a goal to gradually work toward.

Living Your Values

Did you know that research shows it takes an average of at least sixty-six days of practice to build a new habit? Try not to be discouraged if you initially feel awkward. You can add or increase the desired practices into your life at a small rate. Be realistic and kind, and allow your body and mind time to acclimate. LeAnn started out by listening to or reading very short self-compassion recordings on weekends only. Later she added a few weekdays, and months later she added some longer readings. Now she sometimes watches online videos of self-compassion mantras or meditations. She allowed herself several months to slowly build up this practice.

Use this chart to plan how increase new habits over time. The first column refers to what you are practicing from the present moment to one or two months from now. The second column refers to practices you plan to add in three to six months. The third column refers to what you plan to start six months and beyond. As a lifelong learner, you can keep updating and modifying these practices and goals periodically. This chart is available to download at http://www.newharbinger.com/52724.

Plan to Live Your Values

Immediate Practices (now to two months from now)	Midterm Practices (three to six months)	Future Practices (six months and beyond)

Check in with yourself about these practices. What helps you to stay on track? Nurturing and reinforcing our values is something we should be intentional about. What works best can be a little different for everyone. For example, I benefit from having an accountability partner, someone to support and check in with. Jae prefers setting reminder notifications on their phone. Ryan likes to have a physical checklist printed out, so he can check off tasks when completed. LeAnn made an artistic vision board and hung it on her wall. Seeing her values and goals beautifully displayed keeps her motivated.

What reminders or tactics will motivate you to practice your value actions?

_____

_____

_____

_____

_____

_____

With a growth mindset, you are frequently taking in feedback and information to help you evolve. Asking for others' perspectives can be helpful. Whom do you trust to provide healthy perspective or opinions? Check off any of the following and add to the list if you have other options:

☐ Friend   ☐ Teacher/professor

☐ Romantic partner   ☐ Coach

☐ Caregiver/parent   ☐ Spiritual leader

☐ Grandparent   ☐ Therapist

☐ Sibling   ☐ Mentor

☐ Other family member   ☐ _____

When you feel unsure about the alignment of your values with your practices and habits, or you want a little input or encouragement, you can consult with these people.

Finally, what are some centering questions or checkpoints you can establish for yourself to ensure that your actions, choices, or situation are as congruent as possible with your values? Jae occasionally takes a "gut check," a quiet and contemplative moment to sense how their actions feel in their body and gut. When they are feeling coerced or pushed in ways that do not align with their values, their body holds a lot of tension. Ryan asks himself whether he is doing something to "look good" or "look virtuous." This helps him gauge whether a personal sacrifice is healthy rather than enabling. It keeps him focused on what is truly meaningful and prevents him from getting pressured into doing things that seem superficial.

How will you plan to check the alignment between your values and actions?

_____

_____

_____

_____

_____

_____

_____

Rest assured that living your values is a lifelong process for everyone. Investing the effort to intentionally center your values is a big part of paving your own healthy healing pathway. After traumatic events, we sometimes lose track of who we are and how to stay connected to our values. Remember that while everyone has different priorities, you have the right to choose your own path to living yours.

I am excited that you are taking the time to claim your unique identity and taking charge of how you define and live your values.

Chapter 3

Tend Your Bodymind

Asian heritage cultures have long histories of understanding the body and mind as integrated elements, hence I intentionally use the term *bodymind*. For example, traditional Chinese medicine (TCM) practices emphasize the prevention and treatment of illness by protecting the equilibrium of the body. These traditions predated Western medicine by thousands of years. Whereas Western philosophers like René Descartes struggled and debated about the concept of the mind–body "problem of duality," most people of the global majority cultures accept that the body and mind are naturally a holistic, inseparable, interdependent system.

Simply put, harm to your body impacts the mind. When you are injured or sick, you don't think clearly and are more vulnerable to depression. Harm to your mind and emotional state impacts your body. When you are scared, your heart beats fast as adrenaline races through your body. The systems work as one bodymind constantly recalibrating and responding to your environment in an effort to maintain health and equilibrium. Furthermore, PGM cultures honor the ways that your bodymind is connected to your community and the larger natural world. Your bodymind flourishes in a peaceful natural environment and when connected to supportive people. There have even been studies which found that people recover faster after surgery when they have a hospital room filled with plants or providing a view of trees (Ulrich 1984). In 1982 the Japanese government recommended spending restful time in nature, referred to as *shinrin-yoku*, or "forest bathing," which has been correlated with positive antidepressant effects (Furuyashiki et al. 2019). Another powerful example is the evidence that emotionally deprived children experience stunted physical growth even when food intake is sufficient (Rogol 2020). Calories alone without social interaction and care are not enough for optimal health and growth of the bodymind. Researchers have been able to measure the impact of stress hormones on the human body at every level, from our cardiovascular system down to our hair follicles.

High stress and traumatic events cause your bodymind to become dysregulated and disconnected from a balanced state of health. A typical symptom during and following trauma is disassociation. Disassociation feels like a sense of blurring or detachment from reality, like you are not in your own body. During and after disassociation there are sometimes gaps in memory, a sense of unreality, and lack of control. Modern-day pressures like our workaholic culture also obscure healthy bodymind rhythms. Intergenerational traumas such as a legacy of war and colonialism have also saddled many Asian Americans with a sense of disintegration. Traumatic experiences disrupt intuition and integration of natural bodymind needs. As the author and somatic coach Kelsey Blackwell writes, "The path toward healing internalized colonialism requires connecting with the parts of ourselves we've been trained to dismiss and discount"(2023).

Have you ever suppressed your hunger or thirst? Or realized your body was very tense or your breathing was shallow? Have you ever responded to bodymind symptoms with annoyance or impatience rather than with care and curiosity? Pay attention to your breathing, the sensation of your body in this moment. Pause to tune in with your bodymind. Then think of some situations where you did not respond to signals that your bodymind needed care, and write about them.

_____

_____

_____

_____

_____

_____

_____

_____

_____

Ben's experience is an example of how we might not understand the bodymind warning signs of distress. Ben's family were refugees from Vietnam. Ben's dad died when Ben was only two years old. Ben's mom got remarried, but his stepdad became emotionally and physically abusive to the family. Ben coped by stifling all his feelings and overachieving at school. He started a great finance job right after college. He's puzzled, however, that despite having finally achieved a good life, he continues to suffer panic attacks, low confidence, and social anxiety. He is frustrated and mad at himself that small stressors trigger long-lasting spirals of catastrophic thoughts, dark moods, and tension headaches. When he feels bad, he worries and continues to criticize himself, which makes him feel worse. All of this takes lots of time and energy. He often spends his nights and weekends lying on the couch suffering waves of headache pain. After finding that all of Ben's blood tests and scans are normal, his doctor refers him to a psychologist.

Have you ever experienced physical symptoms that were strongly tied to emotional stress, or have you noticed your mental health state impacting physical symptoms? Write about that here.

_____

_____

_____

_____

_____

_____

_____

_____

_____

_____

When you don't feel well, I encourage you to take a deep breath and seek to understand what your bodymind is expressing. Buddhist philosophy states that everyone suffers sometimes, and that this is a part of the natural cycles of life. There is no human life without pain. It's not realistic to be happy and healthy all the time. Nonetheless, you can meet pain with acceptance, flexibility, and compassion to enable yourself to move through it as smoothly as possible. Alternatively, you can react with anger, judgment, or panic, which prolongs or expands the experience of suffering. There are many types of signals that your bodymind may be sending you. Perhaps the symptoms are indicators that you need to see a doctor, get more sleep, stretch your back, eat more vegetables, or find an activity for expressing anger or fear that is being held in the bodymind. Are you practiced in listening to and understanding your bodymind sensations?

Be Present in Your Bodymind

Take a moment to be present and pay attention to the current state of your bodymind. Do you feel tension or pain anywhere? Are you holding on to any stress in your bodymind right now? Where in your bodymind do you tend to express or hold stress? How do you feel in moments of anger, sadness, or fear? Write down the sensations.

_____

_____

_____

_____

_____

_____

_____

_____

_____

_____

You can also draw or write on this body diagram to show where you feel stress.

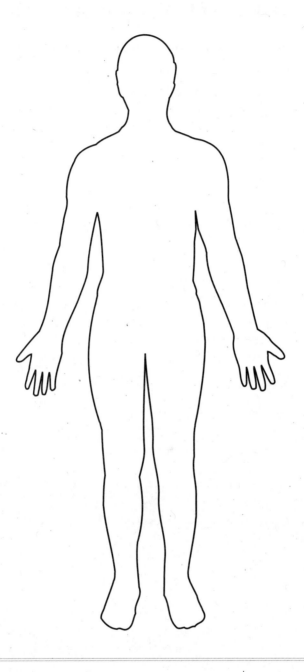

Practice attuning to the sensations and signals of your bodymind. This will provide cues for when to take better care of your bodymind.

Taking Awareness into Care

When there is proper care and feeding for the bodymind, natural healing occurs continually, and you do not have to extend major efforts to facilitate healing. Your bodymind knows what to do. However, if you neglect or ignore bodymind needs for too long, an injury can fester into something more severe, just as ignoring a cut to the skin can lead to an infection. Suppressing and ignoring emotional trauma can be expressed via bodily aches and pains and significant fluctuations in moods and sleep.

This is why self-care is health care. Self-care practices are a fundamental set of behaviors to value and protect your health. As the author Audre Lorde wisely said, "Self-care is self-preservation." The specifics of your self-care plan will be different from anyone else's, because your bodymind has its own unique set of ideal conditions. Engaging in reasonably balanced lifestyle habits will support trauma healing. I intentionally use the word "reasonably" because healthy habits do not require intensive hardcore exercise or severe dieting. Let us get away from "all or nothing" and "no pain, no gain" notions of health. Practicing moderate levels of movement, rest, emotional expression, and nutrition are sufficient for well-being. You can create the appropriate mix of actions, routines, and nourishment to protect your bodymind without going to extremes. Some days you may need rest and hydration to support healing, and other days the best option may be to go for a brisk walk outdoors. Some days it may be hot tea that helps you heal; other days it may be singing your favorite songs, prayer, or eating more protein.

When you take your health for granted, you suppress your wellness needs. This can look like skipping meals or not getting enough sleep when you're busy. It may seem like you are being efficient, but in the long run you risk burning out in physical and emotional exhaustion. Learning bodymind awareness, and how to protect or repair your wellness, is a lifelong process. The amount of sleep, nourishment, or exercise best for optimal health will vary at different stages of your life and depend upon what stressors you face. Young children tend to need more sleep than adults. Teens may need more food than kids or adults. An adult with a stressful job may need to practice stress-reduction skills more often than a retired person would. Seeking environments and activities that support your wellness will positively impact your health. Animals and plants naturally seek out the right sunlight, food, and conditions for their growth and well-being. You too can seek healthy things with intention.

Jojo's recovery story is a good example of someone who had to learn to listen to her bodymind instead of forcing herself to "power through" and ignore her needs. Jojo has always been proud she can pull all-nighters and work harder than anyone. Recently, she was violently carjacked in a grocery store parking lot. She was badly injured and needed surgery, but she jumped back into her hectic work routine as soon as she could after being discharged from the hospital. She was used to taking work home almost every night, but now she feels overwhelming fatigue. Her surgery scars are not healing well. She has urges to bite her fingernails and pull out her hair. Her sleep quality has been disturbed by nightmares. Jojo has noticed her face and shoulders are "scrunched up" and tense. She has also been grinding her teeth in her sleep. Her best friend convinced her to use her workplace benefits to get therapy. Jojo chose a therapist who practiced somatic body-focused skills with her in therapy, and she learned skills for integrating her experiences and self-soothing her agitated nerves after trauma. Jojo's dad encouraged her to get exercise. Although exercising when she felt fatigued seemed counterintuitive, Jojo signed up for pickleball. After a few months, she noticed improvements in her sleep quality. The urges for nervous hair-pulling had dwindled. Her shoulders and gut no longer felt "heavy." Her face was relaxed, and her jaw stopped feeling sore, as she was no longer grinding her teeth at night. Investing time and effort to rest and express herself had supported her healing.

Notice Your Calm Bodymind

Where does your bodymind tend to express joy or calm? How do you feel in moments of contentment? Write down the sensations.

_____

_____

_____

_____

_____

_____

_____

_____

You can also draw or write on this body diagram, showing where you feel joy or calm.

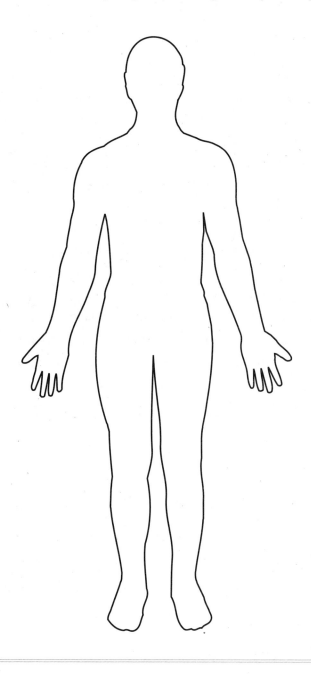

Understanding the Impact of Cumulative Trauma

The impacts of stressors and traumas are cumulative. Experiencing personal trauma makes it harder to handle typical life stressors like financial worries, schoolwork, relationship concerns, and job pressures. In addition, many Asian Americans and other historically oppressed groups in the United States are negatively impacted by social and systemic stressors that contribute to minority stress syndrome and racial trauma. These social and systemic stressors have occurred historically and continue today. Minority stress syndrome describes the way a lifetime of experiences of systemic discrimination, internalized oppression, and encountering prejudice negatively impacts mental health, wellness, and access to health care. Existing as a historically oppressed, targeted, or excluded group creates additional stress load on a person, which is correlated with significant strains on behavioral and physical health. Studies such as the 2007 analysis by Ahmed and colleagues have shown how the constant fatigue of living as a minoritized person and experiences of discrimination increase mental and physical vulnerabilities and health behaviors. A 2011 study by Balsam and colleagues also found that exposure to minority stress is increased for those who live with multiple marginalized identities, for example, as an Asian American who is also disabled and queer.

Racial trauma does not mean that you suffer trauma because of your race or the color of your skin. There is nothing wrong with you being who you are. Racial trauma is created by oppressive and exploitative historical systems like colonialism, in which people in your racial group are subjected to stressors, microaggressions, and attacks that others do not have to contend with. The root of the problem is not our race or culture. Do not confuse being targeted with being the source of the problem!

Here are some life experiences that contribute to racial trauma:

Direct exposure to racist abuse or discrimination. This can take the form of someone threatening you or discriminating against you by denying you a job.

Witnessing abuse or violence toward your racial or cultural group. This can be seeing someone being bullied in-person or viewing news footage of Asian victims of race-based violence.

Witnessing abuse or violence toward loved ones. Many children of immigrants have witnessed their parents being mistreated due to lack of language fluency.

Living with fears about safety. When anti-Asian attacks escalated during the COVID-19 pandemic, Asian Americans nationwide lived with constant worries for personal safety as well as fears that their elders or other loved ones could be violently targeted.

Exposure to racist stereotypes. This can include hearing racist terms in your workplace or having negative stereotypical assumptions made about you, such as an employer assuming all Asians lack assertive leadership skills.

Invalidation and questioning. This occurs when people or institutions do not believe you and question your lived experience, like someone denying that you have been harmed by caste discrimination or racism.

Your health care provider might not assess for or even comprehend the potential health impact of racial traumas and identity-related stressors. The work of psychologists of color such as Dr. Lilian Comas-Díaz (2016) indicate the importance of assessing, understanding, and processing race-related stress and trauma to promote psychological decolonization, support community engagement, and create a social action path to holistic health. This holistic and historical perspective differs from the symptom-focused medical model assessments of mainstream health care.

Whenever you feel unsafe, your bodymind will respond in protective ways. This also means your body may be reacting to feeling unsafe even when there is actually no threat to safety. In an excellent book titled *Why Zebras Don't Get Ulcers*, Dr. Robert Sapolsky (2004) explains that when you feel stressed or threatened, your body floods with stress hormones so as to concentrate energies toward fight or flight. Like other animals, when sensing danger, your standard bodily tasks like digestion, sexual function, cell healing, growth, and immunity are suspended to direct focus on responding to attacks. When you are scared, you may notice the way your heart races and your body will feel jittery. Without conscious effort, your body has prepared defenses against a perceived danger.

Unlike the occasional stress of animal life, human stressors are often chronic, and the negative impact of stress builds up over time and negatively impacts functioning and health. If you have a one-time stressor, your body would react and then return to standard daily functions. However, if you have unpredictable or frequent traumas, the ups and downs of bodymind reactivity become physically and emotionally disruptive. You may end up exhausted, dysregulated, and depleted from hypervigilance. Trauma creates confusion, as your bodymind doesn't know when it's safe to rest. You may be hypervigilant, which is when you are continuously on anxious alert, and may overreact to situations which don't necessitate a full-blown fight-or-flight response. Over time, these chronic stress bodily reactions make you vulnerable to illness. It can be difficult to find the right middle ground, so you can calm yourself so as not to overreact to small things yet remain alert enough to safely live in a world that contains threats.

Nida is an example of someone whose bodymind has become overly agitated and reactive because of traumatic experiences she has survived. Nida's family immigrated to Kentucky from India when she was four years old. She endured racist bullying throughout her childhood and survived sexual harassment from a professor when she was an undergrad. She's now a perfectionistic law student suffering from painful stomachaches and flare-ups of psoriasis and acne. Nida feels self-conscious about her appearance and is losing confidence. She is irritable to everyone around her. Her parents and boyfriend are critical of her lifestyle habits and behavior, which just makes her feel worse. But her grandparents are more supportive. They suggest that her physical symptoms are a normal reaction to intense stress, and encourage Nida to explore bodymind practices to restore a healthy balance.

Developing Bodymind Awareness

Variations of body scan and mindful breathing are popularly taught in yoga and meditation classes. In practicing body scan, you become aware of where in your body you may be holding stress, or where in your body the bodymind needs greater care. In modern life, we tend to focus all our time and attention on thoughts. We can be so much in our head that we're cut off from how our body is doing. At times we purposely treat our normal body needs as something that should be overcome. I want you to reframe this perspective and understand that when your body expresses hunger, thirst, pain, fatigue, craving, or other needs, it's not a flaw. Your bodymind is talking to you by design, as it should. These sensations and experiences are a marvelous natural force to get your attention and drive you to seek what you need to be healthy and well.

If you're new to body scan and body awareness, I recommend starting in small doses. The goal is to bring awareness to your body in a methodical manner. With regular check-ins and practice, you will strengthen your sensitivity and holistic self-awareness.

Mindful breathing is a practice that can be learned quickly and used daily. Once you slow down and tune in to your bodymind, you may notice how oblivious you have been to your precious breathing. Each day we take some 20,000 breaths, about 7.5 million breaths each year (Stephens 2021). How many of them did you truly feel or were you even aware of? Mindful breathing alone is a useful practice for being in the present moment and being aware of your body.

Try Mindful Breathing

Choose a quiet and comfortable place where you won't be disturbed.

Sit comfortably in a position where your body can rest without strain. This could be on the floor or on a cushion with your legs crossed or on a chair where your feet can rest on the floor and your back is supported.

Simply notice the position of your body.

Breathe in, notice how it feels to fill your lungs.

Breathe out and notice how it feels to exhale.

Breathe in a long breath and feel the breath.

Breathe out a long breath and feel the breath as air moves through your body.

Continue gentle, deep breathing.

There is no need to force a breath or count the length of breaths. Some natural variation is okay. You might want to place a hand on your belly to feel your breaths move in and out. Or you can leave your hands by your side. Do whatever feels most comfortable.

If your mind is being very active, release the urge to engage, suppress, or interpret your thoughts. Just let your thoughts drift past you like clouds. Continue to breathe and sit in quiet observation.

As you sit in the moment, check in with your body. Start at the top of your head, and slowly, gently scan the rest of your body. Perhaps as you breathe, you will unclench your hands and lower your shoulders. Tune in to how your body feels, with a spirit of curiosity. Let critical thoughts float past. Where you notice uncomfortable sensations, imagine breathing into them, loosening your grip. Visualize letting go of tension and letting it evaporate and drift away. Move past when you feel ready. Continue to scan all the way down to your toes. Notice the support of your muscles, the energy of your breath. Breathe in appreciation for the composition and activities of your bodymind, as it protects and nourishes you through each day and connects you to your ancestors and this natural world.

Another contemplative bodymind practice for when you have a bit more time is progressive muscle relaxation (PMR). This practice can help you feel present and relaxed, especially at the end of the day and before bedtime. You can practice PMR in bed or sitting up or lying down elsewhere. Choose a safe, tranquil place. You can download a free guided PMR meditation at http://www. newharbinger.com/52724.

Do you have a visual image for your relationship or feelings of bodymind? It can be something personal and unique to you or it can be an ancient image and concept rooted in culture and ancestry. For example, in different parts of Asian cultures, there are representations of the bodymind and its energies using colored chakras, the symbol of a lotus, or a tree of life.

Doodle or draw an image of bodymind here, if you like:

Culture and Our Bodymind

Asian cultural healing wisdom predates recorded Western medicine by centuries and can be compatible with it. For example, traditional Chinese medicine is often complementary to Western medicine in the treatment of chronic disease. Ayurvedic medicine, which translates to "knowledge of life," has long recognized the role of stress in loss of immunity and vigor. What connects these ancient approaches is a view of bodymind health as a holistic system for which we can preserve balance. Some Western healing settings integrate traditions that include bodymind and spirit, such as the Hmong shaman certification program at Mercy Medical Center in California, where patients access medical treatment alongside spiritual shaman care, to maximize holistic healing. Another example of integrating traditional healing wisdom into Western medical care is the Waianae Coast Comprehensive Health Center in Hawai'i; their medical and dental facilities include a Kupuna (elder) council, healing herbs garden, and lomilomi massage.

What do you know about how your heritage culture cultivates good health?

_____

_____

_____

_____

_____

Does anyone in your family use traditional healing practices?

_____

_____

_____

_____

Do you notice the signals your bodymind sends when your stress is excessive?

_____

_____

_____

Nida found a way to blend cultures and care for her bodymind when her grandmother (Nani) took her for consultation with an Ayurvedic healer. The healer taught her methods for steadying herself when she experiences symptoms of imbalance—excess *pitta*, or heat energy. Instead of feeling angry and fighting her body, Nida now pays attention to bodily discomfort and tends to it sooner. Simple changes to her ergonomic workspace and daily breathing patterns have helped her feel better. She notices how cravings for salty and oily foods coincide with hormonal and stress cycles, so she increases hydration and fresh produce at these times to help restore balance. Her Western doctor is prescribing acid-reducing medications and has scheduled her for an endoscopy to investigate her stomach pains. The Ayurvedic healer provided herbs for Nida to use in washes to soothe her skin conditions.

Consider some ways that the whole of knowledge and traditions can be tailored for you. While Western medicines have demonstrated evidence-based excellence in many conditions, they tend not to contribute to long-term balance and can also have unintended side-effects. Many traditional healing methods work more slowly and take lifestyle into account. Then there are health recommendations that are recommended by all: healers and scientists around the world recommend regular body movement, ample sleep, and balanced nutrition.

What are some health maintenance actions you can incorporate into a complementary approach tailored for you?

_____

_____

_____

_____

_____

Researchers have found that it takes an average of two months or so for new habits to stick, and adopting new bodymind health habits could take patience. The good news is you can explore a huge variety and number of actions and habits that are all beneficial. I recommend adding healthy bodymind habits to your life by selecting a few things you can realistically do that are speedy and quick (done daily), some that involve a medium-time commitment (done every week or so), and some long-term habits that either take more time to develop or are done on a monthly or annual basis.

Adopt New Bodymind Care Habits

Adopt some new bodymind care habits by checking off habits that you plan to practice. You can add your own ideas in the space provided.

Daily Habits

☐ Drink water

☐ Deep belly breath

☐ Release your shoulders

☐ Moisturize

☐ Floss

☐ Hug a person or pet you care about

☐ Eat a fruit or vegetable

☐ _____

☐ _____

☐ Stretch from head to toe

☐ Stretch arms out wide

☐ Relax your jaw

☐ Wash your hands

☐ Smell something calming

☐ Wear something comfortable

☐ _____

☐ _____

☐ _____

Weekly Habits

☐ Take a walk

☐ Meditate

☐ Massage

☐ Reduce sugar

☐ Do something creative

☐ Take a social media break

☐ _____

☐ _____

☐ Learn to cook a new vegetable dish

☐ Do weight training

☐ Try a new food

☐ Make time to laugh

☐ Reduce substance use

☐ Enjoy natural scenery

☐ _____

☐ _____

Long-Term Habits

☐ Establish good sleep hygiene

☐ Maintain an exercise practice

☐ Quit smoking

☐ Buy supportive shoes

☐ _____

☐ _____

☐ Get annual health exams

☐ Advocate for healthy community

☐ Take preventative health care measures

☐ Learn a new self-care skill

☐ _____

☐ _____

Keep track of how your bodymind responds to these new practices.

You should feel free to experiment and adjust to what works best for you. Figuring out the right timing for self-care is important too. For example, when Ben joined a spin class after work, he discovered that he didn't sleep well on those nights, so he switched to morning workouts and felt much better. In therapy, Ben learned to appreciate and understand how his body "freaks out" under stress, related to his childhood traumatic experiences. He now practices simple self-acupressure and grounding techniques on days when stress is high. He also practices reciting affirming mantras every morning. He chose the mantras "Past abuse does not define who I am as a person" and "I am breaking cycles of trauma. I am a change maker." These skills, paired with exercise as a physical outlet, have reduced his panicky episodes.

Jojo also recalibrated her bodymind self-care routine. Jojo tried a juice cleanse that a friend recommended, but decided not to continue as it made her feel tired and deprived. She noticed that she sleeps better and feels calmer on the weeks that she plays pickleball and after visits with her family. With family, Jojo laughs a lot and feels replenished from singing karaoke and enjoying home-cooked meals. Jojo used to take pride in being a workaholic, but she was always stressed out. Now she pays attention to small joys on a regular basis and her bodymind is thriving. Jojo knows that if she grinds her teeth at night or starts to bite her nails again, it's a warning that she needs more support and care to stay healthy.

What pattern or schedule works best for you? Do you prefer being active early in the day or later?

_____

_____

_____

_____

_____

_____

Have your needs and preferences for types of food, movement, and sleep changed at different times in your life? Write about those situations here.

_____

_____

_____

_____

_____

_____

_____

_____

_____

_____

_____

_____

_____

_____

_____

_____

Your bodymind is a valuable part of the complete natural world. You are the embodiment of your ancestors, a part of your environment and community, and a precious being deserving of respect and care. It's amazing how your bodymind regenerates new cells every single day, while simultaneously retaining some cells for your entire life. Your bodymind needs will fluctuate with the seasons and years, just like nature does. Using bodymind awareness and care skills and adjusting them periodically will allow healing to occur.

Tending to and heeding the insight of your bodymind is an action of respect and investment in yourself and all that surrounds you. Keep it up! Use mindful breathing and body scans, drawings, and other activities to check your attunement, status, sensations, and needs periodically. In the next chapter, you can explore how to access rational thinking, which works in tandem and synergy with bodymind wisdom.

Chapter 4

Use Reason
to Access
Wise Thinking

Have you ever jumped to conclusions and said or done things you later regretted? Or reacted in a way that made an already difficult situation worse? Reacting before thinking is something everyone does occasionally. As someone who has survived trauma and felt unsafe, however, you might react this way often, and this habit can make life's challenges tougher than they need to be. Emotions have an important functional role in providing information and building intuitive knowledge, yet if you want to make good choices, it's better not to rely on emotions alone.

The solution is not to go to the opposite extreme and try to make yourself into an unfeeling robot or logic machine. You can cultivate steady wise thinking, which is in the middle ground between being overly reactive and overly repressed. Just as chapter 3 focused on finding your balanced healthiest state, this chapter will guide you in finding a route to a measured practice of wise thinking.

From an ancient Buddhist perspective, wise thinking occurs when you can think and respond, without the confusing influence of ego, insecurity, and attachment. It's a state of mind where you can notice and ponder your thoughts and feelings calmly and with clarity, letting go of those that may be unhelpful. In ancient times, being rejected from a community or group might be a life-or-death situation. In modern times, this is hardly ever the case. Your primal emotional mind handles threats to the ego the same way it handles threats to your physical safety. When you feel intensely afraid of people scrutinizing or judging you negatively, this is social anxiety in action. The worries are magnified beyond the reality of the threat level. Needless worrying and defensiveness is distracting and exhausting. If you want to read more about a specific skills framework, Marsha M. Linehan (2014) adapted Buddhist concepts for her dialectical behavioral therapy (DBT) approach. In DBT she encourages the development of a *wise mind* state.

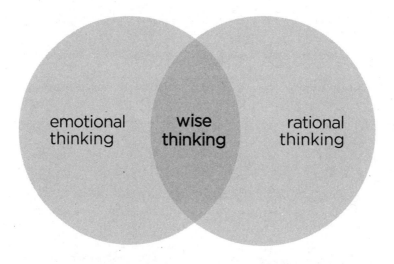

In this chapter you will have a chance to slow down and explore how to apply your reasoning skills in emotionally upsetting situations. Wise thinking is practicing being in a middle space where emotional thinking meets with your reasonable, rational thinking. The idea is to practice examining your feelings and thoughts in a meaningful way. You will reduce impulsively acting out with conduct that makes it hard for you to communicate what you want, or in ways that you will later regret. Think of this as pumping the brakes when you are driving a car. The goal is to slow down, so you don't speed off too far in the wrong direction. You do still consider your emotional and gut response, however. Wise thinking buys you time to recalibrate. It is building a habit to pause and consider before responding.

It is possible to access wise thinking, even if you have been told you have a "sensitive" or "hot" temperament. Even if trauma and temperament have made you prone to reactivity, you can use observation, a slower pace, clear descriptions, logical reasoning, and mindful presence as steps toward wise thinking. Just like the other skills throughout this book, you can build wise thinking by taking small steps. Nobody is born thinking wisely. We develop emotional modulation and reasoning skills over time, and even as an adult, you can hone these skills and improve at any life stage.

You may have heard the popular term *amygdala hijack* in reference to emotionally overreacting to something with intensity that seems out of proportion to the situation. This term was popularized by psychologist Daniel Goleman in his 1995 book *Emotional Intelligence: Why It Can Matter More Than IQ*. Goleman emphasizes the ways that skills in such areas as self-awareness, impulse control, persistence, motivation, empathy, and navigating social cues can be even more beneficial than the kind of book smarts that society usually equates with intelligence. Your amygdala is the instinctive part of the brain that reacts lightning-fast to danger, whereas the prefrontal cortex (PFC) is the part of the brain understood to regulate thoughts, emotions, and behavioral control. It used to be thought that when the amygdala becomes activated, it "hijacks" the brain so that the PFC is unable to do advanced reasoning. Recent research, however, supports the idea that the amygdala is not merely a reactionary, fear-focused part of the brain but has an important role in clarifying the importance of things and engaging in pleasure and joy as well (Dixon and Dweck 2022). Making decisions in a constantly changing world is complicated. Your amygdala and prefrontal cortex work continuously to calculate and evaluate costs, benefits, goals, and safety in dynamic situations.

With this updated view, consider how you can use wise thinking to enhance your emotional intelligence. Wise thinking is a state where all aspects of the brain can interact in a calm and meaningful way. Emotional reactions, such as feeling your heart race or adrenaline pumping, are your bodymind preparing to keep you safe from danger, whether real or imagined. When this occurs, you can use wise thinking to soothe those reactions if they are not accurate or useful. Is someone getting uncomfortably close to you physically? In that situation, wise thinking may conclude that this is definitely a problem, and you should react strongly to preserve your personal space and safety. Alternatively, with wise thinking you can often dismiss upsetting stimuli, like irritating social media posts, which are not actual threats. To be clear, wise thinking is not about controlling reactions but about using experience and logic to tailor your responses for the appropriate time and situation. When you think wisely, you allow troublesome, unimportant things to flow past you. This way, you reserve your attention and energy for higher priority items.

Veena's experience is a good example of how to implement wise thinking skills to improve a situation. Veena comes from a large Thai American family where everyone frequently talked over one another, and her parents often argued in loud screaming matches. Family members had to raise their voices in a struggle to be heard. Now as a young adult, Veena was upset that her partner did not seem to care how hurt she was about something he'd said. When she communicated this, he apologized. He also gently gave feedback that because Veena "yells about everything, no matter how small," it's hard to know what she feels strongly about. Veena thought about this and realized it was accurate. She reacts to even minor annoyances by "blowing up." Veena's friend, who is a schoolteacher, recommended that Veena try pausing before yelling: take a deep breath in, visualize a red stop sign, and ask yourself, "Is this a big problem or a little problem?"

Veena tried this out. Here were the results:

Friend late by ten minutes: **little** *problem*

Cashier at store was aloof: **little** *problem*

Dirty glass in sink: **little** *problem*

Partner's remark that hurt my feelings a lot: **big** *problem*

Misplaced remote control: **little** *problem*

Salad mix in fridge past expiration date: **little** *problem*

Other driver on the road too slow: **little** *problem*

Veena and her partner agreed to both use this pausing skill to assess what things were worth discussing and what things had lower or little priority. When she stopped yelling, Veena found her partner to be more responsive to her needs. She also noticed that "blowing up" less often felt good while driving and going about her daily life. She used to become easily defensive and irritated, argue frequently with random store clerks, and get snippy with her friends. Feeling calmer has made her interactions with other people go more smoothly. Her family-of-origin habit of starting to yell or scream when distressed was no longer useful.

Learn to Pause

Next time you feel upset, take a deep breath and briefly visualize a stop sign in your mind. Ask yourself, is this a little problem or a big problem?

Little problems can be annoyances or minor misunderstandings that don't warrant a big response. In daily life, you may encounter traffic during your commute, poor customer service, spilling a drink, a messy desk, or a friend who is temporarily unavailable, but while any of these problems may be bothersome, none is worth a big emotional reaction that could derail your mood or deplete your time and energy.

Big problems are significant and worth taking time to address. You could employ wise thinking to decide that asserting yourself at the doctor's office, making sure you are paid fairly, or addressing a communication breakdown with a loved one is worth channeling your efforts to prioritize.

Write down a few examples of little problems you have experienced:

_____

_____

_____

_____

_____

_____

_____

_____

Write down a few examples of big problems you have experienced:

_____

_____

_____

_____

_____

_____

_____

_____

_____

_____

Wise Thinking Awareness of Trauma Reactions

As a trauma survivor, your body and brain are primed to be ultra-alert. Having a reactive mental state is common for trauma survivors, including those diagnosed with post-traumatic stress disorder (PTSD). Learning about some common trauma reactions can help you use wise thinking if trauma is at the root of your problematic reactions. People who have experienced traumatic events like abuse, betrayal, or abandonment may feel:

Rage episodes: Prone to intense anger and full activation into self-protective rage, even if the precipitating event is a little problem.

Hypervigilance: Being hyperalert and overreactive even when there is no current threat. This can cause a state of being exhausted, distracted, easily startled, or jumpy.

Dissociation: Mentally checking out is often a survival method to cope with traumatic events. This becomes maladaptive when feelings of depersonalization (like you're watching your body from above and life is happening to someone else) or derealization (life feels fake, like in a dream) makes it difficult to live in and respond to present situations with continuity, emotional presence, and clear thinking.

Intrusive thoughts or memories: Unwanted and intrusive thoughts and memories can interfere with your moods, ability to focus, and ability to be present. When intrusive thoughts and memories are ruminations of frightening or upsetting content, they can disrupt mental functioning and peace of mind.

If you have a reactive mind, or feel easily triggered, you might find it beneficial to consider the influence of intergenerational traumas. *Intergenerational trauma* refers to the variety of ways that trauma experiences in previous generations may have a negative impact on the health and wellness of current and future generations. This does not mean that being a survivor of intergenerational trauma is some kind of inherent weakness or flaw. Survivors of trauma also inevitably pass on traits of strength, resilience, creativity, and resistance. Using wise thinking, you can work out which lessons and habits of the past work wisely in your present, and which do not.

Looking back at your youth, consider whether your caretakers or community members were victimized by political traumas, such as war and genocide, or interpersonal traumas. Trauma survivors can inadvertently pass on some of the impact of their own suffering, and survivors who have not been able to access healing care often behave in problematic ways. If people you relied on, parents, loved ones, or authority figures, were sources of abuse or neglect, you may have attachment trauma, which can show up as disassociation or anxious attachment in relationship situations. Chapter 7 will target relational concerns, but I bring it up now, because as you engage in wise-thinking practices, you might notice that relationship stability and attachment concerns trigger sensitivity and reactivity.

Nai's story is a good example of how attachment issues play out. Nai and his three sisters had a scary, erratic home life. Their parents struggled with gambling addiction and legal problems. There was frequent violence in their neighborhood. The children grew up not knowing if anyone would pick them up at school. They were often hungry and fearful that they would be abandoned. Nai is an adult now and gets embarrassed about how "clingy" he gets when dating. If someone he's interested in doesn't respond to his text messages or wants a little personal space, his emotional mind panics. He has gone on text rants and called the same person a dozen times in an hour. He regrets it later, as potential romantic partners interpret Nai's anxious outbursts as "demanding, creepy, and needy."

Nai has been learning to practice wise thinking and self-grounding at his local temple. A monk has been teaching Nai to decrease the old habits of emotional mind that scare away the very connection he longs for. They've discussed ways for Nai to remind himself of facts over fears and of constructive actions to take when he feels overwhelmed by urges to repeatedly text. Recently, instead of compulsively texting, Nai responded to his distraught feelings by saying a prayer and then jogging in a nearby park. He visualized himself chanting with the monk for a few minutes, and then watched his favorite comedian on Netflix.

The monk from Nai's local temple gave him the same advice that many professional counselors recommend: to practice positive activities that can replace problematic emotionally reactive urges and habits. Emotional reactivity is not inherently bad; it may help you express yourself. But excessive emotional reactivity creates problems. In Nai's case, the habits of becoming demanding and clingy led to social rejection and embarrassment. Nai often felt emotionally overwhelmed because of his childhood abandonment experiences. Yet others interpreted his frantic efforts as controlling and rude.

Here are some common examples of emotionally reactive response habits and the problems they may generate.

Emotionally Reactive Habits	Associated Problems
Ruminating on negative memories or thoughts	Worsening mood, failing to see positive things, agitation
Isolating self	Feeling lonely, rejecting social support, social problems
Taking out emotions on other people (yelling, blaming)	Relationship damage, guilt or regret, family problems, work or legal issues
Emotionally manipulating others	Damaging trust, feeling guilt or regret
Overworking or hypercompetence	Avoiding real issues, feeling fatigue, burnout, lack of communication about actual issue
Excessive fawning, people-pleasing	Becoming prone to abuse by others, failure to offer self-care, being misinterpreted by others as insincere or phony
Self-punishment or harm	Scarring, shame, pain, risks to health and safety
Using drugs or alcohol to manage intense feelings	Loss of money, risk of addiction, poor health, safety risk, legal problems, or relationship problems

Write down any emotionally reactive habits you may have and any associated problems that have come up in the past.

Emotionally Reactive Habits	Associated Problems

How does one think wisely to assess a situation before reacting? As an example, I can use my own experience at a professional conference where several very prominent psychologists were presenting their research findings. I was sitting quietly and noticed that I had started feeling unsettled and anxious to leave the room. I took a few deep breaths and lowered my tense shoulders to quickly relax. Then I mentally "stepped back" into an observing, wise thinking stance to notice what was coming up. Sure enough, unhelpful critical thoughts threatening my ego were present:

Maybe I should have worn a fancier-looking professional outfit.

Should I be worried I was not invited to speak at this event?

Will lunchtime be awkward, as none of my colleagues or friends are here for me to eat with?

Wow, this presenter is so smart. I haven't done research like that.

Will my question sound silly to the rest of the audience?

After noticing these scattered judgmental thoughts, I was able to remind myself of my motivations for attending the conference. I exercised self-compassion, remembering that everybody feels this way sometimes, and it's not a big problem. I could admire another person's work—or their outfit, for that matter—without degrading my own worth! I also recalled past occasions where I had survived awkwardly entering a space without knowing anyone, and chuckled upon reflection that people of all ages still remember the childhood distress of sitting alone at lunch. Thinking this way was calming, and I remained present for the conference. Instead of avoiding discomfort, I examined and dismantled it with wise thinking.

When you encounter a triggering situation, you can use wise thinking to choose actions that are measured and reasoned rather than hasty and emotional. Here's what Sang did when he was triggered at a workplace lunch with six colleagues, including his manager. Someone mentioned that Sang had handled the training of several new staff members, and his manager said, "Just wait until the new employees have to apply what they learned during crunch time." Sang noticed himself feeling unhappy about this comment. He had the urge to say something sarcastic and leave the table, but he took a deep belly breath instead. He realized he wasn't certain about what had pissed him off. He mentally walked himself through these wise-thinking steps before doing anything else.

Describe with facts only: His manager had spoken in a laughing manner. His tone of voice was normal, and he looked calm. Some colleagues chuckled in response.

Notice your thoughts and emotions, and identify and label what you observe: Sang noticed he felt angry and embarrassed, and he started to recall every annoying thing his manager had ever done. He felt anxious and insecure. He felt targeted and like his manager was doubting his skills at training new employees.

Stay in the present: Sang mentally distanced himself from overthinking about every critical thing that had ever been said to him. When he noticed intrusive thoughts about his parents' emotional abuse, yelling that he was useless and disgusting, Sang envisioned letting the past stay in the past. He refocused his attention and thoughts on this single interaction today at lunch.

Stay in your body: Sang noticed his face was still hot. He had initially felt an urge to spring to his feet in a rage. This was beginning to subside. Sang took a drink of water and took another deep breath.

Practice nonjudgment: Sang grew up often being told he "should" or "should not" feel or think certain things, or otherwise he was somehow bad. He reminded himself that judgment is not helpful to learning. He remembered his therapist's advice that there is nothing wrong with his full range of emotions. He was uncomfortable but acknowledged his discomfort without judging it.

Respond in a way that is practical and useful: Sang chose to ask in a calm voice what his manager had meant by his comment. His manager replied that when the new staff hit difficulties, only then would they truly understand the outstanding training Sang had provided.

Assess what occurred: Sang noted that his reactive mind had misinterpreted his manager's compliment as a criticism. This had triggered sudden unpleasant physical and emotional reactions. If Sang had immediately responded with a rude comment and left the table, it would have made the situation worse. By taking a few moments to reflect before responding, Sang shortened the amount of time he felt upset and quickly reengaged with his colleagues.

Use Wise Thinking When You Feel Triggered

Think of a recent situation where you felt emotionally overwhelmed or reactive. Now break down the situation and imagine a wise-thinking response. Write in the space provided.

Describe with facts only:

_____

_____

_____

_____

_____

Notice your thoughts and emotions, and identify and label what you observe:

_____

_____

_____

_____

_____

Stay in the present:

_____

_____

_____

_____

Stay in your body:

_____

_____

_____

_____

Practice nonjudgment:

_____

_____

_____

_____

Think of an action or response that would be practical and useful:

_____

_____

_____

_____

_____

_____

Try this process out in real time when you are feeling emotionally overwhelmed or reactive, and then assess what occurs.

Going forward, using wise thinking will get easier with practice. One way to rehearse these skills is to say or read aloud mantras each day to center wise thinking and calm the tendencies of your reactive mind. A mantra is a brief positive phrase, affirmation, or value reminder that you repeat to yourself for the purpose of cultivating mindfulness and motivation. In some spiritual traditions, a mantra can be a sacred verse or a portion of a longer scripture or important teaching. A cultural idiom can also be your mantra. Starting each day or ending the night with a mantra takes less than a minute. Or you can practice more frequently. My Stanford colleague Dr. Oliver Lin, who teaches a class on Asian American psychological perspectives, recommends saying your chosen mantra thirty times, twice per day. You can connect mantra practice to other aspects of your normal daily routine, like getting dressed in the morning, sitting down to lunch, or while preparing dinner.

Here are some mantra examples. Feel free to use these or come up with mantras of your own. You can draw from cultures and languages other than English if they resonate with you or include spiritual mantras that feel personally meaningful:

I breathe in peace and calm.

This issue does not define me.

I can overcome this.

I can feel anxious and still do what I need to do.

I can let go of things that don't serve me.

I need not explain or qualify myself to others.

This emotion is temporary.

Perfectionism doesn't serve me. I have inherent value.

Nothing is too late to mend (Thai: ไม่มีอะไรสายเกินแก้).

Peace, Om Shanti Om (Sanskrit: ॐ शान्ति).

Everything is difficult in the beginning (Chinese: 万事开头难).

Write your mantras here:

_____

_____

_____

_____

_____

_____

_____

_____

_____

May you keep these mantras active in your daily thoughts and routines, as you apply wise thinking.

Going about your daily life from a wise place is not just a matter of temperament. Despite trauma experiences, you don't have to feel constantly reactive and unmodulated. As you practice activating wise thinking, you will increase cognitive flexibility, the ability to calm and slow down so you can choose helpful actions. Learning ways to handle your thoughts constructively is a path to trying out new and more adaptive actions. Don't suppress the emotional mind, but learn to examine and respect emotions and blend that with rational skills.

In the next chapter, you will learn more about methods you can use to decrease the intensity of negative feelings and experiences.

Chapter 5

Surf Uncertainty to Cultivate Peace

This chapter will help you reduce the rehashing of pain and internalized criticisms that use up your emotional energy. Survivors of trauma and abuse often notice long-lasting damage to their self-concept, sense of safety, and trust. This is at the root of shame and other intensely difficult thoughts and feelings. Unhelpful mental ruminations and overthinking patterns can extend suffering far past the original harmful events. In this chapter, you will learn some ancient mindfulness practices to help you float over the waves of stressors or problems and let them ripple past, so they don't get stuck in your mind and increase your suffering.

These ancient Asian mindfulness practices loosen the grip of ego and overwhelm in response to life's stressors. We all suffer sometimes, but when the ego and our interpretations of events go on overdrive, we suffer more and longer than necessary. Being present and integrating aspects of your consciousness, emotions, and physical sensations are a time-tested path to improved peace and contentment.

Pay attention to what you notice as you practice increasing your attunement to bodymind and wise thinking. It's normal to initially find the experience unsettling. Just because a concept is simple does not mean it is easy to practice! You might have spent months or years avoiding full awareness of your emotions and bodily sensations. To survive, you learned ways to wall off the painful and incomprehensible pieces of your experiences. Humans do this out of self-protective instincts. Mindfulness and self-awareness practice can start off as extremely uncomfortable if you haven't experienced a sense of minimal safety or have low emotion-modulation skills. This is why it's ideal to find comfortable places where you can feel safe and relaxed to practice bodymind awareness. The more you test new perspectives and examine your internal experiences and sensations, the easier and smoother it will feel. Your strength and growth potential are far greater than you realize.

With the work you've been doing in this book, you've already started to liberate yourself from internalized oppressions. Famed educator and philosopher Paolo Freire wrote extensively about a "conscientization" process of growth, where critical thinking can increase your awareness of oppression, internalized and external, and move you to prioritize freeing yourself from others' domination. Simply put, you've been pulled into harmful games that you no longer have to play. Internalized oppressions as well as memories of past pain can render emotional modulation difficult. Now it's time to explore practices for reducing the impacts of the past, and choosing to presently focus emotional energies in healthy ways.

Letting Go of Old Hurts

Can you think of some examples of things from long ago that remain hurtful in your mind? For example, most of us can still remember someone saying something really mean to us when we were just a small child. Here are a few more examples:

Jake still feels pangs of rejection when he remembers always being the last kid chosen for sports teams during physical education classes.

Emily's abusive ex-husband constantly criticized her appearance and told her no one else would ever love her. She knows now that she deserves love and a kind partner, but the cruel comments still replay in her mind.

Fang's fourth grade teacher humiliated her in front of the whole class for speaking Cantonese instead of English, and Fang still burns with shame and anger at the memory.

Manny's father is already dead, but Manny still feels like he has to "prove" his worth to his judgmental dad.

Do you have past hurts or insults that you are still replaying in your mind and heart? What are they?

_____

_____

_____

_____

_____

_____

_____

Now visualize setting old insults and harmful thoughts aside. You might never completely forget the hurtful memories, but I invite you to practice reducing the impact they have on you. Can you visualize what to do with these old harms? Some examples include:

Setting your past hurt on a paper boat to float away

Putting the constant worrying in a mental "parking lot"

Leaving the hurt on a shelf: still present but not something that you need to touch frequently

Writing down compassionate comfort words to your past self

Writing the hurt down on paper and then shredding it

Can you think of some other examples to reduce the energy and attention you give to old hurts?

_____

_____

_____

_____

_____

_____

_____

_____

_____

_____

_____

Cultivating Equanimity

Let's explore how to be present in a state of equanimity. *Equanimity* is an ancient value, even though it's not frequently spoken of in modern times. In Buddhism, equanimity (Sanskrit: *upekṣā*) is a fundamental mode of being. Equanimity is not a feeling or a specific way of thinking or a religion. It is usually defined as a sense of mental calmness, composure, and steady temperament. With equanimity, you don't avoid reality even when it's difficult. You also do not prolong suffering by interpreting, blaming, or obsessing over something. Equanimity is steady, conscious acceptance and a clear-eyed way of engaging reality and all of life's fluctuations.

As you cultivate equanimity, you will find that the opinions of other people and random occurrences in life will no longer fundamentally change your experience of reality, and of yourself. Imagine being in a state where flattery, criticism, or attempts at manipulation wash past you instead of impacting your emotional life. Imagine that someone is dumping their anger or insecurity onto you by saying mean things, but you can let the hurtful words go by rather than replay them in your mind. Or perhaps an accident occurs: you break a dinner plate, or your car gets a flat tire. These are unpleasant and disappointing situations. When you are practicing healthy emotion modulation, these events may briefly upset you, but you are able to quickly shift to problem solving and resuming your day, rather than allowing upset feelings to replay over and over in your mind. The stressor or problems that occur are merely things that plop into your day and create small waves.

So far, you have been nurturing your unique identity roots, living aligned with your values, engaging the cognitive skills of wise thinking to evaluate situations, and attuning to your body. Using wise-thinking logic reduces the negative thought spirals that stress can trigger. Chapter 4 focused on shifting away from outdated overthinking habits as well as purging problematic stories and narratives from your mind. In this chapter, you will fine-tune what you've learned by exploring and building habits to help you emotionally manage difficult situations. Whereas earlier we were examining the powerful impact of thoughts, now we are building distress tolerance, the equanimity to pass through stressful times.

I bet you're familiar with the frustrating experience of when you know something is not worth being upset over yet you can't stop obsessing about it. That's an uncomfortable state, but it's a good sign that you are noticing what's going on. Noticing gaps between your logical mind and your triggered reactions is an important step, as it indicates where to focus your equanimity practice. The two skills we will focus on here are *emotion modulation* and *distress tolerance*: the first reduces the intensity or duration of strong emotions, and second helps you accept and survive distressing events without panic, rumination, or self-destructive reactions.

My Stanford colleague Dr. Oliver Lin provides an example drawn from his commute to the office during a particularly stressful time in his life. He would get flustered when cut off viciously by another driver and noticed it would put him in a bad mood well after the drive was over. It was as if he had internalized the harsh energy of the negative interactions and carried it into the rest of his day. Oliver chose to use a hybrid of positive affirmation and mantra work to draw emotional energies away from the negative incident. His actions are not painting a happy face on a bad incident, but rather are acknowledging "I'm so flustered when cut off by the other driver" and then moving on to repeat the phrase "but this does not define me at the core of who I am." He repeated the mantra thirty times at three separate intervals (usually paired with meals) each day, even on days when he was not commuting to work. This approach is simple yet powerful. Research supports that positive self-affirmations reduce negative ruminative thinking.

Why so many repetitions? In classic mantra meditation, a person repeats a sound, phrase, or thought until the practice induces a near-empty state of mind where anxiety or "noise" falls away and the mind feels calm. For both physical and mental movements, when we rehearse healthy proper moves over and over, we can eventually do them without much conscious or intentional effort. When you are less intensely impacted by these events, being calmer allows you more space to think and be intentional about how you choose to respond in the moment. You become able to respond with intention instead of reacting in panic or impulsively.

Practice Affirmations and Mantras

Write down some affirmations and mantras you can practice to reinforce your emotion modulation. I hope you grow to love and accept yourself wholly. If you have experienced very harsh treatment and harsh internal thoughts, this may feel awkward. It's also okay to practice neutrality instead of full positivity if that feels more comfortable.

Think of an upsetting situation that can get you feeling "stuck," rehashing or ruminating negatively.

_____

_____

_____

_____

_____

_____

What can be a self-affirming reminder for yourself in that moment?

_____

_____

_____

_____

_____

What mantra can you rehearse that will help you pass through the upsetting situation?

_____

_____

_____

_____

It helps to review and practice at regular times during your day. Oliver chose mealtimes. You might choose waking or bedtime, at the end of the workday, or during a snack break. When is a good time for you to take a few moments for practice?

_____

_____

_____

_____

You might silently review your thoughts anywhere, or you may prefer a private place to say the words aloud or a quiet place to write. Where can you practice?

_____

_____

_____

_____

You may have a certain way you prefer to practice. Oliver verbally repeated the phrases to himself thirty times. I personally like to write things down on paper with a pen. How do you prefer to practice?

_____

_____

_____

_____

How would you like to respond with intention and choice?

_____

_____

_____

_____

_____

_____

_____

When a strong emotion seemingly arises out of nowhere, we can learn to reflect upon it with compassion. Hannah's story provides a good example. Hannah's mom relies on her as a translator and lifeline, whereas Hannah always feels like a disappointment to her emotionally abusive dad. She's constantly putting a positive smiley spin on situations or apologizing in interactions. Last week, when she "exploded" in a tearful rage at a friend, everyone was shocked. This was so out of character for her. Hannah's church mentor advised her to think about what had contributed to this oversized reaction to a small thing.

Upon reflection, Hannah recalled that earlier in the day, her friend had given her a tip for how to increase her daily exercise. She thanked her friend for the tip but over the next few hours grew increasingly hurt and angry. Hannah kept thinking about what her friend had said, assuming it meant that _I am a fat loser, hopeless, and ugly, just like dad says._ Later it all blew up in a rageful outburst. Hannah was embarrassed and confused. She chose to practice self-affirmations, mantras, and wise thinking analysis to help understand her reactions.

One of the striking elements of Hannah's story is that she was embarrassed that she felt hurt, which caused her to suppress her true feelings and pretend she was fine. Her embarrassment is an example of a _meta-emotion_: the feeling you have about your feelings. The fact is that everyone has difficult and sometimes illogical emotions. This is normal. Yet when we start to be mindfully aware of unhelpful thoughts, we sometimes make ourselves feel bad or guilty about feelings. Life is already challenging enough—no need to add another layer of judgment on yourself! Remember the goal is to observe and understand, not deny, suppress, or judge.

Having self-reflection is a great skill for us as inherently social animals. Yet when we experience trauma, racism, sexism, ableism, homophobia, classism, or all the other negative things which impact us over time, we internalize that negatively biased gaze. So it's important to note that we are seeking a balanced state here, a little self-reflection, without blame or judgment alongside it. Whenever you notice the meta emotions happening, I want you to visualize a red stop sign!

Stop beating yourself up with judgments about your emotions. The approach I want you to learn here is to notice your troublesome emotions or thoughts—not to judge them, but to learn to turn down the volume and surf past them.

How to Surf Emotional Waves

Constructive coping skills can help you surf waves of pain and uncertainty in life. You may have never had specific education or training to build these skills. Some modern elementary and high schools now have social-emotional learning classes. Graduate business schools feature fundamental courses on self-reflection and interpersonal communication. At every level of education, there's now increasing awareness of the benefits for self-modulating skills. But if you had no such exposure, that's certainly not your fault. Indeed, exposure to traumatic events may have created so much distraction, disassociation, and agitation in your life that your bodymind was preoccupied with survival.

Every human life will have some indignity, inevitable disruptions, disappointments, and suffering. In recent times, our communities were certainly tested mightily by the impact of what felt like unending waves of traumatic uncertainties during the COVID-19 pandemic. There was economic insecurity, social isolation, death and grief, illness, fear, and constantly changing policies, alongside what the Center for the Study of Hate and Extremism reported as a 339 percent rise in anti-Asian hate crimes in 2021. Most of us have never seen so much uncertainty and misery in our lifetimes. You might still be grieving, angry, or fearful. Over time, a lot of us felt exhausted, sometimes panicking at every new and unprecedented turn of events. In such times of crisis, it's important to have a realistic understanding of the facts and to avoid becoming overwhelmed or panicked.

When thinking about all the things that happen to a person during a lifespan, I visualize an ocean. The oceans are vast, natural, and essential aspects of our world, perhaps the source of all life. The oceans are powerful. Some days the waves are comforting and pretty. Cozy waters swish around your ankles, and the waves are fun to splash in. You can think of this as the swirl of staying busy in your life. Other days the waves get rough and loud. Some seasons the waves become icy cold, huge, and potentially destructive. Think of these as the waves of life events that are out of your control.

When the waves are difficult, there is no choice but to learn to live with them. These waves may be small, such as experiencing the personal biases of people we know, or they may be huge, such as wars, economic crises, or natural disasters. We cannot avoid or halt the waves on earth or in our lives.

But you can learn to surf the waves. The wisdom of the ancients applies here: you are decreasing feelings of blame or attachment.

Have you ever watched someone surfing in the ocean? The very first step is to just watch the waves. This is what you have been doing using wise thinking and bodymind awareness. Observing the turbulent areas where you often experience trouble aids you in judging how to plan your approach. To take the ocean analogy a little further, surfers start by sitting or kneeling on the board in shallow waters. It takes an optimistic attitude and some patience with the learning curve before they can begin to stand and balance on a surfboard. Even after they stand, they must remain alert and responsive as they ride the wave.

I invite you to build a sense of being in equanimity, of cruising and balancing through life's waves. Sometimes they are to be expected, and you will see them coming. Other times, such as with COVID-19 and the rise of Asian American hate, you will be surprised at their appearance, impact, or scale. Overall, it is far better to learn to surf than to stand on the shore getting repeatedly clobbered. You can't hold the waves back. It's also okay to have feelings about the waves. I am certainly angry and sometimes scared and full of grief, yet I also know that after honoring my emotions, I can adapt to this reality.

As you learn to surf, you will continue to get splashed. It can be scary, and, yes, sometimes you will fall off the board. Practicing equanimity is a good life skill to protect your peace and can even become fun. One of the sensations I hope you can regain is exhilaration—that feeling of pressing yourself to go outside your comfort zone or of being a little scared, yet persisting in building your emotional tolerance and self-efficacy. Surfing, or going beyond your usual comfort zone, releases endorphins and adrenaline, which can make you feel present, very alive, and in the moment.

Practicing Surfing

In *No Mud, No Lotus: The Art of Transforming Suffering*, Thich Nhat Hanh (2014) wrote that mud is a necessary organic part of life. It appears ugly and dirty, but mud nourishes the lotus to develop into a beautiful, versatile, and valuable plant. When the lotus flowers wilt, they become compost and return to mud, which will ultimately nourish new blooms. The lesson is that messy and unpleasant parts of life are essential to creating the parts we value. I am not advising you to indiscriminately accept and tolerate all terrible things that happen to you. There are situations when you should set boundaries and push back. We will examine boundaries, self-advocacy, and empowerment mindset in chapter 8.

Acceptance and commitment therapy (ACT) teaches us to understand, accept, and be more flexible in responding to life's difficult situations and the negative feelings that arise. One skill from ACT to practice is referred to as *cognitive defusion*. This refers to developing the ability to notice our thoughts, reactions, and sensations, so we can learn to observe and defuse automatic judgments or triggers. Defusion can help you let go of meta-emotions. One of the most powerful ways to do this is by using a brief bodily calming skill and then walking yourself mentally through your thought process.

You can also try some other methods:

Noticing. Simply noticing what is happening can help you defuse an emotion, as it offers perspective. It allows you to take a few steps back.

Naming the emotion. You might say "that is really disappointing" and set the emotion aside once the feeling is labeled.

Humor. Sometimes engaging with difficult feelings in a funny or irritating voice or character helps you to not take it too seriously.

Picture a fishhook. Let the "hooks" pass by you in the water—no need to grasp at the feelings and get hooked.

Distancing. Imagine putting the troubling thoughts and feelings in the next room or even farther away to diminish how much of your attention they take up.

Another ACT skill is *acceptance*, learning to live alongside unpleasant feelings, urges, and thoughts without expending struggle, undue attention, or judgments. Do you notice the common practices that ACT borrows from Asian philosophies? We still use ancient tools for modern concerns.

Let's see how Alice applied a cognitive defusion technique when she was visiting her family and sensing a wave of annoyance rise up. Alice immigrated to New York with her family from Beijing when she was twelve. She's now a financial broker in her thirties. She sought therapy when her fiancé almost broke off their engagement. He said he loves her but fears they will never be happy together as her daily complaints and misery felt "impenetrable." She was bitter that her parents chose to immigrate into the crowded, low-income shared house they had lived in. She was furious at the racist bullies and cruel teacher that humiliated her as a child. She was resentful that her younger siblings acculturated more easily than she did. She was scared after getting mugged at a bus stop. She was pissed off at a negative comment from a coworker.

Alice realized that accumulated resentments from the past were piled onto and poisoning her present. It was true she had reasons for being angry. Yet ruminating on these events overshadowed the positives: a loving fiancé, a lively circle of friends, an interesting and well-compensated job. She was determined to find better ways of dealing with life's problems and to forge a happier future. Instead of allowing herself to be pulled into waves of emotional upset, Alice decided she would try cognitive defusion.

During a family visit Alice's parents said some critical invalidating things. She felt intensely annoyed. She thought, *I can never satisfy my parents.* These thoughts and feelings usually triggered a cascade of bad feelings and memories. When overwhelmed with bad memories, she would often get into an argument. During this visit, however, she simply noticed, *I am having the thought that I can never satisfy my parents.* She washed her hands in cool water. This grounded her body in the present moment. With cognitive defusion, she was able to notice her thought and create space to choose her response. Acknowledging the thought and noticing her annoyance from a distance allowed Alice to disengage from conflict. She remembered that her parents' have pre-existing emotional struggles and that it's pointless to get hooked into debates and arguments.

Much of what bothers us is lack of certainty and lack of control, because it can feel threatening. It's therefore important to develop a healthy sense of what is and is not in your realm of control. Also it helps to know what is and is not in your realm of responsibility.

Surf the Waves

Use your senses to customize what helps you modulate your reactions to difficulty or uncertainty. Perhaps it's visuals, perhaps it is spoken word poetry, perhaps it is music, affirmations, sutras, scripture, metaphor, or movement.

Alice came up with this list of metaphors to repeat to herself when she feels triggered:

Surfing on waves

No mud, no lotus

Bamboo plant bends, not breaks

Stone worn smooth but solid

Shelter during the storm

Write down the metaphors, music, or other inspirations that can aid you in surfing uncertainty and difficulty better.

_____

_____

_____

_____

_____

_____

_____

_____

_____

_____

_____

Continue to use the practices in this chapter to develop greater equanimity: using your inner wisdom, providing liberation from undue outside influences, and allowing you to grow in both self-compassion and compassion for others even during uncertain times. Refine your abilities to avoid suffering that is avoidable and unnecessary. Every human being will encounter times of illness, loneliness, grief, anger, and fear as a natural part of experiencing new things and growth. Let's nurture the skills to care for ourselves and surf atop the normal waves of change. You can decrease the habits of ego, stubbornness, or fear that bog you down in the difficult waters and mud. Consciously purging yourself of internalized oppressions and external pressures is also a form of protecting your peace and managing uncertainty. In the next chapter, you will concentrate on cultivating healing and wholeness.

Chapter 6

Recover Wholeness

You are worthy of growth and repair to your bodymind in ways that extend beyond mere survival. You deserve to flourish. The thoughtful efforts you have extended while exploring this workbook are investments to restore your rightful wholesome existence. You are already complete and enough, and you have what you need to heal. There are ways you have suffered harm in the past and ways that you currently suffer, which is why you are making the time to rebuild and rebalance. This chapter offers perspectives, skills, and activities that can help you direct your energies and efforts in restorative ways.

Understandably, you may desire or crave approval, but you do not need it. You do not need permission. Weaving together an identity and life defined by and supporting wholeness is the process of healing. Reclaiming your history, story, voice, and place in this world is key to restoring what trauma has led you to cut off or lose. You have been gathering tools for healing in these pages and begun practicing these skills in your daily life. Whether you receive approval, permission, or recognition from others or not, it is significant and powerful that you are taking an active role in your own healing.

Another good nature metaphor is bamboo. Yes, I know bamboo for Asians may seem a cliché! There are excellent reasons that bamboo is beloved throughout Asia. Like the lotus, it provides both food and precious material resources in addition to beauty. Bamboo is known for great strength, versatility and usefulness. It bends in strong winds rather than breaking and is crafted into buildings, furniture, and décor, and even serving utensils. Initially when growing bamboo, no visible sprouts or growth appear for a long time. It can seem like you are lavishing attention on your garden without any obvious growth or gains. Yet under the surface dirt, bamboo is known for growing a wide and robust network of roots. It takes strong roots to support big growth up top. You can't see any of this developing, but when bamboo has been properly nourished, it suddenly grows at an astonishing pace. The lesson here for you is to be patient as you invest in healing your foundational roots. Even if no one notices—even when you may have a hard time seeing your own growth—know that each step you take moves toward the growth that will come from properly cultivating yourself.

Living and Flourishing

You deserve to live in a state that well-being experts and positive psychology practitioners refer to as *flourishing*. There is not a precise measure of flourishing, but the understanding is that flourishing is a state that is balanced and meaningful. It's a view of health that includes growth, belonging, and purpose, not merely the absence of disease. Whereas traditional Western diagnostic definitions of mental health have been centered on measuring the presence or absence of specific symptoms and functional activities, flourishing is a more holistic perspective. Flourishing offers a multidimensional understanding of wellness and contentment. It includes symptoms and activities, but also important factors for your well-being, such as interest, values, hope, and community.

Your goal for wellness is not just to reduce symptoms and go to work functionally but to grow a complex perspective that includes satisfaction and creativity and supports your values and culture. You may have too few symptoms or too little impairment to qualify for a mental health diagnosis, yet you may not be flourishing because of environmental or social factors or a lack of purpose and meaning. Alternatively, even with a mental health diagnosis or other illness, you can flourish if you have a strong sense of life purpose and connection with others. Here are some examples of how this can play out in real life.

Thirty-one-year-old Weng flourishes in important ways in spite of many life stressors. Weng is taking real estate classes, solo parenting her daughter, and working full time as a concierge in a busy hotel. Weng's husband was murdered two years ago during a robbery. She still has nightmares and feelings of unreality that he is gone. Working too many hours, not getting enough sleep, and grief are taking a toll on her health. She is fatigued, gets headaches, and has episodes of feeling intensely fearful. However, Weng's therapist noted that despite these intense stressors, Weng has community support and personal strengths. Weng feels love and daily joy from her daughter, is highly motivated, and remains optimistic that eventually her hard work will pay off. She has family nearby and friends from church that visit and occasionally help with childcare. Weng feels a sense of purpose and belonging in her community. She is an example of someone with high stress and symptoms who also enjoys belonging and flourishes.

Thirty-year-old Christina functions well but does not feel that she is flourishing. Christina is a top seller at her auto sales job and competes in local weightlifting competitions. She is popular for her athleticism and sales skills but feels increasingly restless. She doesn't like her coworkers. Weightlifting used to be fun but now comes with tons of performance pressure. Christina wonders if she would be happier at a different auto dealership, in a different city, or if she went back to school and changed careers. She has casual friends to work out or drink with, but they don't understand her values or share any interests outside of these activities. Her family lives a ten-hour drive away. Christina functions at a high level in terms of how much money she makes and how physically strong and healthy she is. However, she feels aimless and lacks hope that things will improve. She is irritable and frustrated that her activities don't provide fulfillment. Christina is lonely for close connection and is an example of someone with high levels of functional and physical health but who has a low sense of belonging and flourishing.

Are You Flourishing?

Following the research of VanderWeele (2017), there are six primary dimensions of flourishing. These range from meeting your basic material needs to finding a sense of purpose and meaningful deep relationships. Write down what you are satisfied with, as well as what you feel needs growth and improvement, in each of these dimensions by responding to the following questions:

1. What feels satisfying, and what needs improvement, for your sense of happiness and life satisfaction?

    _____

    _____

    _____

    _____

2. What feels satisfying, and what needs improvement, about your mental and physical health?

    _____

    _____

    _____

    _____

3. What feels satisfying, and what needs improvement, for your sense of meaning and purpose?

    _____

    _____

    _____

    _____

4. What feels satisfying, and what needs improvement, to live in ways that support your chosen virtues and character?

     _____

     _____

     _____

     _____

5. What feels satisfying, and what needs improvement, in your close social and familial relationships?

     _____

     _____

     _____

     _____

6. What feels satisfying, and what needs improvement, to support the stability in terms of material and financial resources?

     _____

     _____

     _____

     _____

Looking over your responses to the above questions, how are you faring? Are you functional yet not flourishing, like Christina? Or are you suffering from stress yet still feeling hopeful and connected, like Weng? Where do you flourish in your own life and what areas could use improvement?

_____

_____

_____

_____

_____

_____

_____

_____

How are you doing now compared to other stages in your life? For example, when I was a graduate student, I performed well in terms of academics, work, and volunteer leadership. My body was agile and energetic. However, I was constantly stressed, deep in debt, insecure about my future, and every week felt like survival mode. I think of that phase of my life as high performing but not flourishing. More than twenty years later, my body is far less energetic and agile. I function well, albeit no longer at the sleepless, hyper pace of my youth, yet I now feel inspired by my work. I feel secure with a supportive family and community and a loving life partner. This life stage has serious responsibilities and worries. Nonetheless, I flourish.

Flourishing encompasses the way both positive and negative events may exist simultaneously. Perhaps you are presently financially strained yet emotionally healthier than you were earlier. Or you may live with a chronic health condition while also engaging in exciting and meaningful work.

Do you feel satisfied with the changes and stage of flourishing you are in now, or are there clear areas to improve? Write down your thoughts about your flourishing over time:

_____

_____

_____

_____

_____

_____

_____

_____

Taking a moment to reflect upon your internal sense of flourishing is important because it uncovers the imbalances of your current state.

A Prescription for Radical Healing

All too often we get confused by the powerful messages of society or family about what is "good" or "healthy," and we lose understanding of what is authentic and essential to our flourishing.

Boon received praise for donating to temple and dating a woman from a prestigious family. *His family boasted about this regularly. Boon felt uneasy in his heart. Why didn't he feel the love or happiness his family expected? Upon reflection, Boon realized the monks were not honorable at this temple; they had mistreated him as a child. The woman he was dating did not share his values or interests. She was beautiful and popular but not kindhearted. He had made choices to please his family, but he felt empty and troubled.*

Janice has always been a "good Filipina eldest daughter." *She cares for her five younger siblings, does house chores, and continues to live at home after college. With her new job, she contributes money to the household. Lately Janice has had massive arguments with her parents over their insistence on staying in touch with an uncle who molested Janice's little sister Rona. Their parents would be embarrassed if the kids refused to attend big family events; they feel it would be best if Rona could "forget about it" and that their extended family never know about the molestation. Janice has refused to cooperate. She has set strong boundaries to never allow the uncle near Rona or the other kids. Her parents are now accusing her of being unreasonable and breaking up their family. Janice is not used to defying her parents, and she feels guilty, yet she believes that to protect the kids and help Rona heal, she must prioritize safety even if it confuses and upsets the elders. While this role isn't easy for Janice, she is flourishing by being true to her values.*

There will be times when others will criticize your needs and conditions for safety and healing. This is when it is vital for you to reflect upon others' feedback and wisdom but ultimately learn to center what your own bodymind and wise thinking are telling you. Sometimes community traditions are key supports. Other times you will have to discover or customize new avenues to fulfill emotional, spiritual, physical, and communal needs that your family or community won't understand. You may have to create a blend or mix of practices and wellness habits to suit the complexity of your intersectional identities and values.

What are the core features for your healing and flourishing? Research by multicultural psychologists Mosley and colleagues (2020) supports the idea that mental health treatments are more helpful when tailored to be personally relevant to your cultural preference. Their model of *radical healing* is about reducing individual suffering and including culturally appropriate communal and ancestral healing. This can include political activism to change oppressive systems, intergenerational storytelling, and empowerment through knowledge and reclaiming what has been misrepresented or stolen.

There are four key aspects for radical healing:

- Understand history

- Embrace ancestral pride

- Envision possibilities

- Create meaning and purpose

Let's explore how these apply to your own experiences.

Understand Your History

Chapter 1 addressed the foundational importance of reclaiming your unique identity. Understanding history helps you dismantle lies and stereotypes at the roots of internalized and external oppression. Part of reclaiming a complete sense of self and ancestral pride is correcting the misinformation we have been deliberately and systemically taught. Throughout history, biased and power-hoarding legacies of oppressive systems like colonialism or patriarchy are designed to make you feel insecure. As you learn to critique historical misinformation and conditioning, you expand to define yourself. When you recognize your unique place within the world, you can slowly learn to treat yourself with compassion and curiosity rather than punitive judgment. You can also develop resistance and immunity to further indignities, manipulations, microaggressions, and other insults to your well-being.

What have you learned about your ancestral history? What have you learned about your community history? If you note that there is not much information here, then perhaps this is an area where you can prepare to increase your knowledge.

_____

_____

_____

_____

_____

_____

_____

_____

Embrace Ancestral Pride

Learning about our long histories of resilience, resistance, creativity, and adaptation builds pride in the richness of our ancestry. There are clear mental health benefits to feeling pride in your cultural heritage and identity traditions. Remember that you are a future ancestor as well, and investing time to heal is a precious gift for future generations and those around you. Write down some values or traditions you can take pride in from your ancestry. These can be as simple as the sound of words in your family language of origin, or a fashion or architectural design, or as complex as entire systems of governance and philosophy.

Envision Possibilities

I understand it feels daunting as you journey to a healing place that is unfamiliar. All too often those of us who have experienced traumas are seeking a stable and secure reality that we may never have seen before. It is indeed challenging to navigate without a map! However, your unique healing route combines your reflections, observations, learning, and hopes to create a new road map. It's okay if you begin envisioning possibilities by identifying what you *don't* want to repeat or experience first. At a psychotherapy conference in 2021, Dr. Helen Neville described *radical hope* as "the steadfast belief in the collective capacity contained within communities of color to heal and transform oppressive forces into better futures, despite the overwhelming odds."

I envision a balanced place where you will feel contentment at least most of your days; a future where you feel respected and comfortable in your body and at ease with your thoughts; where you can be collaborative and unafraid in community. Write down some of what you might feel or see in a healthier, more whole future for yourself and your community.

_____

_____

_____

_____

_____

Create Meaning and Purpose

Life in modern times often feels like a frantic competition for limited resources like money, luxury status symbols, or acceptance at elite exclusive places like famous colleges, clubs, or workplaces. Many people who achieve or hoard these things eventually find that they do not bring a sense of peace or lasting satisfaction. You might realize that you seek external goals for others' praise rather than your own fulfilment. Think about what feels meaningful and good in your life. I've heard people identify such activities as rescuing a cat, donating books at a little free library, helping elderly relatives go shopping, teaching someone a new skill, taking care of family, or getting politically involved. Each of these widely different activities created a sense of internal purpose for someone.

How can you live in ways that are aligned with your values and help you feel purposeful within your chosen family and communities? If you feel unsure how to answer this, it may indicate this as an area to build up.

_____

_____

_____

_____

_____

Assessing Your Coping Strategies

Good coping strategies are an important part of recovering wholeness. I know for a fact that you already have coping skills. You've come this far in life! It may be time to take an honest look at whether some are outdated or even harmful. You are a resilient person who has survived difficult situations, and there's no need to feel embarrassed or ashamed if some of your coping skills are unconstructive.

A common reaction to difficult emotions is self-harm, including cutting, skin-picking, hair-pulling, hitting the wall, biting, or scratching yourself. Other common reactions are drinking alcohol excessively or using other drugs, feeling compelled to seek constant excessive noise, gaming, gambling, shopping, exercise, sex, or companionship to distract yourself. Seeking these strong sensory activities is often in the service of avoiding the baseline sensations or feelings. Survivors of trauma often suffer from substance abuse or fall into addictive behaviors as attempts to numb or escape from pain.

Perhaps your way of avoiding emotions is to take something praiseworthy to an unhealthy extreme. Among Asian Americans, the model minority myth and our historical insecurity have caused many in the community to prize workaholism. Everyone has some unconstructive tendencies. As your healing expands, you will be able to tolerate and remain present for a more extensive emotional range of experiences.

Being mindful of balance can help you measure and modulate your coping responses. Just as we previously explored bodymind balance, you can examine your range of behavioral balance. There are many common spectrums of normal, even adaptive actions that can become unproductive and harmful when taken to extremes. Here are some common examples:

Work/school: A healthy relationship to work or academics is when you feel productive, effective, and have some balance with work time and other areas of life. An unhealthy relationship with work and school could be completely ceasing to work or study, or devoting all your time and energy to work at the detriment of all other activities.

Substance use: A healthy relationship with substance use is when you are safe, there is little to no harm in the amounts and frequency of use, and your use feels overall positive. In unhealthy substance use, you may feel unable to control the amount and frequency of use, may use in dangerous situations, and may suffer from hangovers or other negative social, financial, or health impacts.

Sexuality: In healthy sexuality you can feel sensual, experience pleasure, comfort, and safety. Unhealthy sexuality could include a complete shutdown from your baseline sexual feelings or risky hypersexuality and overuse of pornography or masturbation.

Appetite and eating: With a healthy appetite you have a desire for moderate amounts of food and occasional treats, and your eating habits do not take up too much time. Unhealthy eating habits can look like severe calorie restriction, binges, purges, or spending excessive time obsessing about your eating habits.

Body-focused coping: In healthy bodily coping, you may occasionally bite your nails, skin pick, or pull hairs, and it is not bothersome, painful, or disruptive. Unhealthy body-focused coping ranges from being utterly disconnected and disassociated from your body to spending a lot of time and feeling unable to control modes of self-harm even when the result is painful and embarrassing.

If you find yourself at or moving toward an extreme end of a behavior spectrum, it's a useful warning sign that you are getting out of balance and need alternative action or more support. For example, Boon noticed that he drank too much and spent too much money and time shopping whenever he started to get depressed. He chose to cope differently. He was able to reduce his shopping and drinking and substituted going to comedy clubs with his friends and cousins. Janice skipped meals and picked at her skin and hair to the point of causing noticeable damage when her anxiety was high. Now she intentionally seeks to eat some comforting food like soup and use fidget toys instead of harming her skin and hair. She is replacing self-punishing actions with balanced and soothing actions.

How Are You Coping?

A normal behavior for coping or soothing ourselves can become out of control when it is used to an extreme. This can be in the categories listed above or in other things like shopping, gambling, tobacco use, exercise, and sleep. What are your coping strategies, and where are you on this range of extremes now?

_____

_____

_____

_____

_____

_____

As you reflect on your observations, use your awareness to seek more balanced actions for coping. What positive coping behaviors can replace less healthy ones?

_____

_____

_____

_____

_____

_____

Pause whenever you are under stress, and choose a positive coping response. Keep a list of positive coping responses handy, and periodically reassess your coping responses, using what you have learned in this exercise.

Ceremony and Symbolism

To maximize our ability to live in wholeness, we must step away from the rational, quantifiable world at times. Integrating our daily rituals with ceremonies such as prayers or wearing symbols of faith can be a powerful practice. Perhaps you practice with a ceremony during Lunar New Year, Diwali, or Songkran. You can also construct small rituals that center you when you feel unmoored to "come back to yourself."

Here are a few examples:

Christina started to wear the jade bracelet from her late grandmother. *It helps her to feel connected to her culture and the caring she was showered with as a child. It reminds her of Grandma's love.*

Boon put a Thailand sticker on his car and his water bottle. *He feels pride in his heritage, and seeing the stickers reminds him of his larger community.*

Janice cooks arroz caldo the way her grandmother did. *She finds comfort in the delicious food and memories of her grandmother.*

What are some small rituals or symbols which may support your wholeness?

_____

_____

_____

_____

_____

_____

_____

_____

Here are a few examples of medium-to-large actions:

Inez takes a few minutes to send a prayer to her ancestors. *Her heritage is Native American and Pilipino, and she prays in gratitude or when seeking guidance. On the momentous occasion of moving into a new home, Inez made offerings: burning sacred plants, throwing corn pollen, and mano po, asking for and receiving blessings from her elders.*

Boon fasts and prays whenever he has a major life decision coming up. *His fasting and prayer is under the guidance of a new temple he attends. He is now practicing Tonglen meditation to increase compassion to all.*

Janice takes her siblings to a community festival every spring. *There they can feel connected to the cultural foods, art, and entertainment of their heritage without being around harmful family members.*

Weng made an altar for her late husband. *She taught her daughter to burn incense, leave fruit offerings, and share drawings or other new items there for Daddy to "see." Weng modeled ways that they could continue to talk to him as they grieved and moved into new life stages.*

What are some medium-to-larger rituals you can do to support your wholeness?

_____

_____

_____

_____

_____

_____

_____

_____

_____

Construct a Resilience Trophy Case

I want you to construct a resilience trophy case. It can be a physical space like a tabletop at home, it can be a journal with gratitude notes, or it even can be a collection in your mind. Keeping a record or visual reminder of positive things, good days, and prior accomplishments or support can help you weather hard times. You may have a trophy case with awards and trophies, from athletics, art, or academic competitions, but now consider what you would place in your emotional-support trophy case.

Here are some things others have put in their trophy cases:

> Christine has a toy action figure of a strong woman, as it reminds her of all the strong role models in her life.

> Inez has figurines of saints that remind her that her family is always praying for her.

> Weng keeps a dried rose from her late husband and a clay donut that her daughter crafted, as these items remind her of deep love and purpose.

> Boon keeps every thank-you email, note, and card he has ever received from family, friends, and colleagues. They remind him that he is appreciated, even on days when he feels discouraged.

What items would you place in your emotional trophy case?

_____

_____

_____

_____

_____

_____

_____

Recovering Wellness Is Ongoing

There will be times when you feel stuck or broken. During those challenging times, remember that you can heal and grow despite setbacks and injury. As long as you live, you are capable of growth and recovery. Healing and growing are lifelong processes, not something that is completed at one time. Just as you snip off the ends of your hair as healthy new roots appear, you can let go of old thought habits and defensive emotional styles as healthier behaviors, thoughts, and emotions take root. We constantly integrate new growth as our bodies and minds adapt to current situations. When you have your down days, spend some time with your emotional trophy case, and engage with the personal ceremony and symbolism that resonates with you.

As you heal, you will find a sense of self that trauma may have kept obscured. Healing will not mean you become invulnerable. Some difficult things will eventually happen in every life, but you can face the world from a more centered place of wholeness. Also know that the impact of our hurts and traumas are real and substantial, and the time it takes for grieving and mourning are to be honored. Ultimately, the traumas are not you.

Protect your own flourishing as you grow into a radical healing journey. Utilize the wisdom of your family traditions and ceremony and incorporate that into your personalized coping plan. In the next chapter, you will examine how to find connections and belonging in community.

Chapter 7

Gather in Community

This chapter will guide you to foster beneficial connections that are protective of your healing. Community and connection are powerful supports for overall health and happiness. Human beings have always relied on one another for care, survival, teamwork, fun, delight, and bonding. Contrary to the pressures of workaholism and stoicism, interdependence and connection are innate and natural. You are part of the world community. You have a rightful place, or multiple places, in the world of humanity and the natural universe. When a family or community is functional and flourishing, it's easier for you as an individual to feel healthy within it. When you are in good health and flourishing, it's easier for you to be a positive presence and influence within your family and community. In reciprocal networks, you can give and receive with your community and environment. Learning how to cultivate healthy relationships and experience joyful connections is a part of your healing journey.

We are designed to be in connection and community, and our social connections can be amazingly protective of health. For example, feelings of connectedness in school have shown long-term mental health benefits. A 2019 study by Steiner and colleagues found that adults who had said they felt socially connected as middle and high school students later experienced less substance abuse, less suicidal feelings, fewer mental health struggles, and less risky sexual behaviors than adults who felt disconnected in their youth. Social interaction is so necessary that the United Nations has declared solitary confinement of more than fifteen days to be a form of psychological torture. Prolonged isolation hurts overall health. Loneliness has been correlated with increased risk of heart disease, increased risk of stroke, increased risk of dementia in older adults, and overall risk of premature death.

You have probably had periods of feeling disconnected. Perhaps you feel disconnected right now. You are not alone even when feeling alone. Nationwide surveys indicate that declining numbers of adults report having close friendships. A Pew Research Center study conducted by Parker and colleagues (2018) found that only 16 percent of survey respondents reported feeling very attached to their local community. US Surgeon General Dr. Vivek Murthy has deemed loneliness a national public health crisis and created a National Strategy to Advance Social Connection. You can read details about the widespread health impact of loneliness in the 2023 *Our Epidemic of Loneliness and Isolation: The US Surgeon General's Advisory on the Healing Effects of Social Connection and Community*. In 2018, Britain appointed a national minister of loneliness, and Japan appointed one in 2021; each is tasked with reducing widespread loneliness. Declines in connectedness worldwide are negatively impacting health.

How Your Sense of Connection Evolves

Your bodymind is created in connection with family in the context of the larger culture and community. Your attachment to others began in infancy, and it continues to develop throughout your life. You might find that your community and sense of belonging are steady lifelong connections, or you might find that relationships evolve and ebb at various periods of your life. Loneliness can also worsen following traumatic experiences, and this changes relationships as well. Have you felt relationships shift related to your trauma experiences? Do you feel replenished in your hometown, or is a different place more restorative for you?

_____

_____

_____

_____

_____

_____

_____

_____

Depending on your experiences, you may feel solid belonging in your family of origin, friend group, or birthplace, or you may have had to distance yourself from people or situations that were harmful. I want to emphasize that there is no single right way for a family or support community to be structured. Furthermore, connections and community support are not always where we expect them to be. Sometimes those you relied on most can become a source of harm and disappointment. Alternatively, even minor acquaintances can have a positive impact. Research by psychologists Gillian Sandstrom and Elizabeth Dunn (2014) has demonstrated clear mood benefits of even "weak ties" in our lives. Their work illuminates the ways small interactions such as a friendly wave from a neighbor, chatting with a grocery store clerk, or a smile exchanged with a stranger can boost our positive feelings. It's beneficial to make connection wherever you can find it.

Intersectional Community Identity

As Asian Americans, our place of belonging can feel elusive, as we are not wholly a part of our heritage countries and communities, and we also have life experiences and connections that are different from other Americans. Our intersectional identities mean that we find and create connections for our interests and values from mixed and multiple sources.

Asian cultures, and most people of the global majority cultures, are collectivistic. In collectivism the key principle is that the needs of a group should be prioritized over that of the individual. Various Asian philosophies uphold that family, community, and other group roles are more important than individual personhood. This is expressed in different ways and practiced to varying degrees. A simple example is when you drive to an event that is inconvenient and far from home because it is more convenient for others to meet at that location. A larger example is choosing to give up personal resources or delay your own goals to contribute caretaking for an elderly or disabled family member. Navigating cultural nuance can be tricky. For example, your family may expect you to be quiet and defer to elders in the family yet also commend you for independence and assertiveness in the workplace. Expectations and demands are multifaceted and more complex depending on your overlapping identities and roles.

Each of us has a different constellation of roles and relations. For example, both Linda and Sara are twenty-four-year-old Korean American cisgender women, but they prioritize different things in life. Linda wrote that her primary roles in relationships or community are as a fiancée, daughter, best friend, and leader of a dance group. She also sees herself as a global citizen with responsibilities to work for environmental causes. On the other hand, Sara wrote that her primary roles in relationships or community are as the eldest sister, the caretaker of grandparents and younger siblings, and the manager at her workplace. She sees her duty as focusing on the family and relieving her parents' stress.

Linda and Sara have completely different priorities in their relationships to family and community, yet both are satisfied with their connections and roles.

What Roles Do You Fill in Relationships?

Think about the relationships and connections in your life. What are the most prominent or important roles you have among these relationships? Write about them here.

_____

_____

_____

_____

_____

_____

_____

Keep these relationship roles in mind throughout this chapter. As you examine the functions of community and which relationships matter most, you will explore how your current roles are working for you.

Psychologist Lou Felipe (pers. comm.) described a traditional example from her community: "In Filipino culture, the social value of *bayanihan* [spirit of civic unity and cooperation] is often depicted by a community coming together to physically lift and move a *bahay kubo*, a traditional Filipino home, from one place to another. This cultural value is seen throughout history, such as through community action to address the impacts of natural disasters, Filipino migrant labor strikes in Hawai'i and California to improve work conditions, and in the 1986 People Power Revolution against a Philippine dictatorial regime. The *bayanihan* spirit is a way for Filipinos to share their individual strengths, abilities, and knowledge for the betterment of the collective, a necessary approach in harrowing times."

Our community connections exist not only in our family homes and friendship circles but also within the larger context of villages, cities, country, and history. Connections can be acquaintances, loving, familial, romantic, spiritual, political, collegial, ancestral, companionate, or any combination of these factors. Early Asian immigrants enacted mutual care and survival networks such as the Chinese *hui*, Korean *kye*, and Japanese *tanamoshi* lending circles, which made it possible for immigrants to fund a new business or life in a new place. Beyond financial support, our predecessors also created networks to care for one another's families, clans, and even proper care and repatriation of remains after death.

How Do You Engage with Community?

To gain a clear understanding of how you currently engage with community, make a check next to any of the following statements that describe your understanding or experience:

You have responsibility to others.	Individual needs are most important.
Being a rule-breaker is irresponsible.	Being a rule-breaker is good.
You need to consider what others think.	You need to not care what others think.
Your identity is based upon your family or group(s).	Your identity is based upon your individual determination.
You are family- or community-made.	You are self-made.
Your family taught you to be interdependent.	Your family taught you to be independent.
Seeking to fulfill your duty and obligations is important.	Seeking independence and autonomy is important.
You trust group decisions.	You trust your individual decisions.
You were encouraged to adjust yourself to fit in with family or community norms.	You were encouraged to express and validate yourself as an individual.

As you probably guessed, the responses on the left column represent values from more collectivistic cultural norms, and those in the right column represent values from more individualistic cultural norms. As Asian Americans, it's common to find ourselves with a mixed relational style where you check boxes on both sides. There's not an objectively better way of relating, but as with most things, establishing a balance is a healthy path to take.

Trauma might have led you to believe there are no safe people, or to question whether you have a place or value in a community. Harmful people purposely undermine your confidence to strengthen their power over you. Many survivors of trauma report that the emotional, relational, and internal wounds from traumatic experiences are more painful and slower to heal than physical wounds. Hypercapitalism, hypercompetition, and excessive individualism may have led you to a path of isolation and insecurity. You need not be perfect to deserve love and care. You should not demand perfection from others; nor should you idealize them. To be fully human necessitates making peace with the fact that we are all imperfect. Do not despair if your life experiences have deprived you of opportunities to learn and practice emotional intelligence and social connectedness skills. You can seek different opportunities now. You are not doomed if you were not born with strong social awareness, intuition, or communication skills. In his research, Stanford psychology professor Jamil Zaki (2019) has shown that empathy is in fact a skill we can build. There are numerous books, videos, and coaches available to help you build skills in this and other areas of social and emotional awareness. You will find some books listed in the resources at the end of this workbook. Some of the skills from earlier chapters about using wise thinking and emotional surfing can be applied to relating to other people as well.

Holding the Complexity of Relationships

Cultural standards and media entertainment convey ideas that there's a correct way to be a family or community. But there are endless variations which may be equally functional and good. If you don't have a family or friend group that looks and acts like the idealized ones on television, that's okay. Hardly anyone does! Many folks do not feel emotionally close or safe around their family of origin, may not find a life partner, may not want to marry, may not want children, may not have a best friend, or may not attend an organized house of worship or be a member of a social club. Choosing where you invest your time and emotional energies based on societal expectations often leads to emptiness or unsatisfying, insincere connections. Relationships don't have to involve heart-to-heart talks, displays of affection, or frequent contact to be healthy bonds. Sitting beside someone while fishing, cooking, or driving is also companionship. It's also normal for relationships to fluctuate over time. For example, after I moved away from my parents' home, our interactions became less frequent, but my appreciation of them has grown. Alternatively, I've had dear friends grow distant as circumstances and priorities changed. A relationship does not have to last forever to be valuable and meaningful.

Different people and environments will meet different needs. A single family member, romantic partner, best friend, or mentor cannot meet 100 percent of your needs or share identical values and interests. Hoping that they will is an unrealistic expectation. As an adult, it isn't possible to grow and flourish relying on a single person or two, and being around people who have separate life experiences and perspectives from ourselves is a significant part of how we help each other develop. Different people, settings, and activities can provide the connectedness for flourishing. Seeing and accepting the complexities of your relationships with others frees you to flourish and engage within a complex world. Your connections may be different from your home culture. You might find your closest friendships with people of a different race, religion, or socioeconomic background from your own. You may feel contentment or joy with a pet, in a special place, in an online community, or even via a fandom or someone's artistry. Wherever you find comfort or healthy connection is valuable and valid.

Let's look at some diverse examples of how people find community supports and types of connection:

Anh is grateful for the teachers, counselors, and mentors who point out opportunities and nourish her development. Her parents do not support her dreams, but others see her worth and capabilities.

Other fire disaster survivors on social media are helping Ronnie learn about healing and rebuilding. He feels reassured by their posts of practical tips and life-affirming advice. His cat Dolly has been a sweet comfort during the worst times of his life.

Dr. Ramani holds onto ongoing connection with her late great grandmother, grandmother, mother, and sister as she goes about daily life. Knowing their spirit and struggles helps guide her through present-day challenges and in laying the foundations for the next generations.

Jip was devastated when their father kicked them out for being transgender. They moved from Arizona to New York City for college with zero financial or emotional support. Jip made friends in college who also identified as LGBTQ+ or as fierce allies. This community provided Jip with love and understanding. Their college counselor connected them to financial and health resources.

Volunteering at the local animal shelter and attending AA and GA groups has helped Mike heal from alcohol and gambling addictions. These experiences have been a lifeline while working toward recovery and reconciling with his family.

Now take a few minutes to check in with your body and think about where or with whom you feel a sense of connection.

Identify Your Connections

Include all that comes to mind in response to the following questions. As an example, you can see how thirty-year-old Pilipino American Ronnie responded.

With whom do you have the most frequent contact or feel the closest connections? (Ronnie wrote: "My parents, sisters, and my best friend since high school. My girlfriend Arlene. My favorite relatives Tia Joy and Tito Jojo. My grandmothers. One lives with us, and the other lives in Manila.")

_____

_____

_____

_____

_____

_____

_____

What connections are present in your life but not in your inner circle? (Ronnie wrote: "Friends from Naruto fan fiction group whom I have known for eight years. My favorite coach at the gym is a friend. Friends from my office. The kids I mentor at Boy Scouts. Extended family who live in other cities or in the Philippines. College buddies I visit sometimes.")

_____

_____

_____

_____

_____

_____

What connections are not a close part of your life, but are important? (Ronnie wrote: "My role model/idol LeBron James, because he rose from nothing to be successful and also gives charity back to community. Celebrities Lea Salonga and Dave Bautista, who make me proud as a Pilipino American. My dog Toto and I have neighborhood friends at the dog park.")

_____

_____

_____

_____

_____

_____

What connections are not a person but are something else? (Ronnie wrote: "I still think about my grandfathers regularly, even though they are both with God now. My rescue cat Dolly sleeps beside me every night. My dog Toto. The ocean at the beach in Pacifica. I've been going there to think and be with nature since I was in high school.")

_____

_____

_____

_____

_____

_____

As you review and reflect upon the connections you just wrote down, what do you notice? Do you feel like the time and energy you invest is supporting your connections well? Write your thoughts here:

_____

_____

_____

_____

_____

_____

_____

_____

_____

Clarifying your connections can reveal paths of action or acknowledgement. You may notice more appreciation for certain connections. You may notice gaps where you would like to build stronger connections. Are there connections you would like to spend more time cultivating? Perhaps there are people you enjoy but have not contacted in a while, or other people you would like to get to know better. Conversely, you may notice that you would like to prune your social circle. Is there someone who consistently fails to reciprocate your care? A group of friends who seem draining or increasingly irritating? Perhaps you will invest less energy in those spaces.

Explore Where You Feel Most Connected

Do you notice any patterns for what helps you feel positive connection? Perhaps you notice you are most at ease in an online community or in a particular social setting. As an example, I have noticed that when I do volunteer activities, I meet people whom I like and admire, as we are engaged in activities that reflect shared values. Write down what you notice about the places, people, or activities where you feel the most connected and authentic.

_____

_____

_____

_____

_____

_____

_____

_____

Are there activities, traditions, or rituals that deepen your feelings of connection? These could be annual holidays or cultural and social events, or they could be something you do privately. Write down what these are, and remember to engage in them regularly.

_____

_____

_____

_____

_____

_____

As you look over your responses, you can gain clarity about the special types and combinations of places, people, and activities that create community connections for you. Make a conscious effort to take care of your connections.

Be intentional about where you spend your precious energy and time. Social norms have misdirected our community into an overreliance on academic achievements or financial success as top priorities. As a result, you might overwork and neglect yourself, and you may also neglect relationships. We are led to believe that working hard can achieve safety, love, and belonging. Yet sometimes the more achievements and money you attain, the lonelier and more misunderstood you feel. A tendency to overperform, to the detriment of your health, is a fairly common trauma reaction. Community is not about objects or status; it's about being seen, feeling heard, and sharing experiences. It's about the dynamic energy of communication and understanding between people. Strength, care, and resources should amplify when shared in mutual support. It is also the sense of confidence and peace that happens when you feel seen and valued by others for reasons more permanent than your accomplishments. Healthy relations do not require you to perform or prove your worth.

Being fully healed or feeling on top of things is not a prerequisite for connection. I think here of the Japanese philosophy of Wabi Sabi, which accepts the simple fact that everything in life, including humans, is imperfect and in an ongoing state of flux. Our goal is for goodness, for effort and learning, which is not perfection or performance.

You can find meaningful connections in unexpected places:

Indian American Lila feels inadequate and sad after family events. *Many of the elders shame her and hurtfully push dieting advice upon her. They compare Lila's career and car to that of her wealthier cousins. She has no desire to be competitive with her cousins. She loves her family and wishes they could enjoy celebrations together without harsh judgments and comparisons. Lila unexpectedly found community at salsa classes, where everyone is encouraging, even to newcomers. At salsa school, people of all races, income levels, and sizes are joyfully accepted as beautiful. From her dance community, Lila has gradually developed close friendships outside of class. She values family connections for cultural reasons and out of love, but her salsa community provides wholehearted acceptance and joy.*

Vietnamese American Anh found healing outside of her family of origin. *Anh is a successful pediatrician. No one sees the pain she has suffered due to childhood physical and emotional abuse, and she won't talk about these experiences. She grieves that her parents never received help for the wounds of their own traumas and instead inflicted them on the family. Anh has received care and support from teachers and mentors as well as healing validation from her therapist and close friends. Recently, Anh joined the advisory board of a child-abuse prevention organization. Contributing to the community in this way has helped her heal.*

Connections Across Generations

People of the global majority have ongoing connections with ancestors and generations beyond the present. You are always connected to ancestors, future descendants, and a larger community and environment. You utilize wisdom, skills, and values from your ancestors in current life situations, whether you are aware of it or not, and your decisions and actions now have an impact on future generations. When you address your hurt and misinformed beliefs, you build healthier foundations for all that is around you. When you shift harmful patterns caused by intergenerational traumas and oppressions inflicted upon previous generations, you create a gift to the people of the future. I periodically remind myself that I am a future ancestor, and that perspective reminds me of the wisdom and values I seek to actualize. The Filipino Mental Health Initiative of San Francisco holds gatherings under the theme "Kapwa is Medicine," in which prayer, honoring ancestors, and exercise are shared as communal healing.

What intergenerational relational patterns and norms are practiced in your family or community? How do people interact? Who influences one another? Are there examples or role models you want to emulate? Are there examples of relationship behaviors you want to change for future generations?

_____

_____

_____

_____

_____

_____

_____

_____

_____

Ying's story is an example of the types of actions or traits you may examine about your family or community. Ying is a fifty-one-year-old Hmong American woman. She was born in a refugee camp, and her family moved to Wisconsin when she was a toddler. She wants to preserve the humor, generosity, and work ethic of her community. Ying also loves the cooking and embroidery traditions she learned that have been taught for generations. She's proud of her family's survivance story, rebuilding their lives in the US and helping newer refugees. Ying speaks out against the high rates of domestic violence within her community. She and her husband have taught their children skills for healthy relationships so that future generations of Hmong families will break cycles of trauma and violence.

Identify and strengthen your community values with practice. Writing, reading, and reciting affirmations for community building helps root you in the values and hopes and determination you hold for community.

Here are a few community affirmations you can use or adapt to make your own:

I make a difference with the small kindnesses I share.

I accept opportunities to meet new people or have new experiences.

I am not alone in my struggles and gains.

My community can guide and support one another.

I accept advice and help when needed, and share advice and help when asked.

Mutual support and aid make life easier for us all.

I will treat others as I would like to be treated.

I will be treated with respect as I respect others.

I will find connection from multiple sources.

Write down some affirmations here. These do not need to be complicated. Any statement about how you want to connect with community works:

_____

_____

_____

_____

_____

_____

Read and recite your affirmations daily as you grow in your community. Review and update them as time goes by. Notice when your actions or surroundings fall out of alignment with your community values and steer yourself back on track. Notice when a relationship or situation causes you to feel inauthentic or fragmented. Move away from those situations to seek places you can be seen, accepted, and valued as a whole person.

You probably noticed that the topic of community and importance of connections intersects with earlier chapter themes such as tuning in to your bodymind, using cultural practices, and working toward living the values that bring you purpose and peace. Moderation and balance, rather than extremes, in relationships are correlated with contentment and well-being.

Beyond ourselves, our connections with the natural world, creatures, and other humans hold us. In collectivistic values, the ultimate search for meaning brings us beyond ourselves to a wider connection of *cultural perpetuity*, the cultural values and lessons we play a role in passing on beyond our own lifetimes. There is an importance in having time to be alone and reflect, and there is also a vital importance to connect and lean on others as well. Every human needs support at some point. We can provide aid, lending strength and sharing empathy. There's a synergy about what we give and take in relation to others in this world and through generations.

Chapter 8

Empower Your Tenacious Self

We have talked about the importance of grounding yourself in your values, solidifying your identity, trusting bodymind cues, restoring and adapting traditional wisdom, applying wise thinking, and connecting with community. It may feel like a lot of steps to remember and practice. It's normal for new thinking styles or health habits to start out feeling clunky or awkward. Like learning how to ride a bicycle, cook a dish, or drive a car, it takes practice. Eventually you will gain a sense of ease, where something that began with lots of reminders and intentionality will become background flow as you continue on your healing journey.

This chapter will help you on that journey to reclaim your own strength, vitality, and power. Catastrophic and historic events have scarred many of our family lines over the generations. Yet through it all Asian families have expressed a fortitude for survivance. Do not be fooled into believing that feeling pain, suffering, having doubts, or anxiety are signs of weakness. These are normal fluctuations in life and responses to painful situations. The task of each generation is to create the proper balance of tradition and growth and the right pace to maximize healing and nurture our collective strengths. It is your turn to empower yourself with the tenacity to consistently protect your values and well-being as well as the well-being of your community.

What Self-Empowerment Means

To empower yourself is to understand your own growth potential and strengths and to use that knowledge along with your values to make informed choices. You foster your own empowerment by being motivated to learn and asserting yourself to make good decisions. Making good decisions involves applying wise thinking to calmly assess situations and tolerate short-term discomfort, or rebuke, for long-term benefit. For trauma survivors, it can mean the uncomfortable work of venturing into actions that are based on more than just survival and self-protection. Developing self-empowerment can feel unfamiliar if you've previously had to focus all your energies and attention on surviving.

I acknowledge that you have had painful experiences when others withheld validation, blessing, permission, or recognition from you. You have had painful experiences when someone belittled or mocked your experience. All humans long for recognition and support, starting in infancy and lasting through our adulthood and elder years. All too often, the environment or those near us are too damaged, distracted, or unwilling to provide this level of support. In addition, systems around you will sometimes actively manipulate, distort, or deny your reality. I hope that you find a community that sees you and wholeheartedly supports your growth. Yet you can begin this journey even without others' support.

You empower yourself by maximizing conditions and choosing actions that move you toward what you want in life. The process toward empowerment can be difficult, but the result is that you feel liberated and capable.

What Does Empowerment Mean to You?

Take a moment to reflect on what self-empowerment means to you right now. Have you seen positive examples of empowerment? Do you have a goal that would help you feel more empowered? Write about whatever comes to mind.

_____

_____

_____

_____

_____

_____

_____

_____

_____

_____

_____

You must grant yourself permission to make your own life choices. You can start the process by asking yourself where internal desires or needs have not been met. Seeking our rightful wholeness and health is not the same as being demanding and selfish; please remember this when others try to guilt or manipulate you into surrendering all your needs. Every living creature is meant to seek a healthy existence. As Asian Americans we consider cultural and community values too, and empowered choices balance these individual and collective factors. For example, I have personal life goals that include meaningful community work and sharing with my family. I have learned that I cannot support others' very well, however, if I am not attending to my own mental and physical health first. Ultimately, empowerment that nourishes your flourishing also models and reflects health back to others. Caring for and healing yourself brings healing into your community.

Self-Advocacy and Healthy Boundaries

As you make your own life choices, you will need to employ self-advocacy and set healthy boundaries. As an Asian American, you might feel unclear about how to assess the health of your boundaries. Asian heritage families have different ideals for boundaries than Western therapists and communities do. Balanced collectivism, extended family support, and community care are the norm in our ancestral countries. However, an extremely distorted version of collectivism has sometimes resulted from colonialism, misogyny, ageism, and casteism. These problematic norms demand the self-sacrifice or denial of personhood. For example, some Asian families demand complete self-sacrifice from mothers and eldest siblings or condone mistreatment of less abled or younger family members. It is important you know that expressing loyalty, gratitude, and care is not equal to agreeing with every single request or command.

Sometimes the most loving action we can take is to choose what is healthy and wise over what is convenient or customary. Boundaries help preserve relationships by improving clear communication, establishing authenticity, modeling healthy relationships, avoiding resentment, reducing manipulation, and limiting burnout. Traditional Asian values do glorify the idea of self-sacrifice but also encapsulate that everybody shares sacrifices and care—not that certain family members burn out completely. If your health is destroyed, it not only is miserable and unfair to you but also renders you unable to help and function in your roles to your family and larger community. A skill in mature boundary assertion is to develop a sense of what is healthy and empowering in the big picture. This includes healthier ways of speaking and thinking to yourself as well as to others. Self-advocacy is learning to understand, appreciate, and communicate your needs. Boundaries are the space where you can have care and love for others while also demonstrating care and love for your values and self.

Depending on the circumstances, setting a boundary may mean protecting your energy and engagement. To use a sports analogy, you're protecting yourself and your perimeter as defense. In another scenario, you may actively assert your needs and self-advocate. Continuing with the sports analogy, this would be your offense, when you raise your needs and move forward. This not only helps you but also helps others. The common saying "You can't pour from an empty cup" applies here. You cannot truly help others without also providing for yourself.

So how can you learn to do this better? Examining and observing healthy boundaries and self-advocacy skills can help you develop your own.

Twenty-three-year-old Burmese American Hayma found inspiration in the movie *Titanic*. *She specifically resonates with the character Rose's decision to rebel against a forced marriage for money to a horrible person. When Hayma's widowed mother put intense pressure on her to marry Steve, a wealthy but mean-spirited man, Hayma refused. She asserted that she would choose her own life partner. Refusing to commit her future to someone she did not want to be with was the first time Hayma had ever disobeyed her mother. It was difficult, but she knew her life would be filled with regret if she gave in.*

People in Vinh's Vietnamese American community were badmouthing his big sister Lan. *She had filed a criminal complaint for sexual harassment against her boss, Mr. Tran, an elder leader in their city. Their parents were mortified at the publicity and described Lan's behavior as "ungrateful and embarrassing." Lan stated that she was not Mr. Tran's first victim, and that she must stand up for herself and others. Vinh, who is eighteen, views his sister as brave and truthful. Vinh and Lan are now collaborating with other young adults to speak out about abusive elders in the community. Vinh's parents think their kids are being rude and ungrateful to the community. Lan and Vinh assert that they love their community and are therefore protecting it by exposing abusers and ugly secrets.*

While Hayma and Vinh's situations were very different, they both exemplify how your values provide the foundation for self-advocacy and boundary setting. Equally essential is understanding your emotional health needs, which can be all too easy to overlook. You might be so busy with work and other responsibilities, for example, that you lose track of your own wellness needs.

Let's look how thirty-year-old Korean American Sean approached this problem. Sean is a married US army veteran, now working in marketing. Sean faced intense racial bullying from peers when he was a child, and his father died when he was ten. Later he experienced combat trauma as well as sexual harassment from a fellow soldier. His whole life has felt unpredictable, cruel, dangerous, and unfair. Sean has PTSD and suffers from sleep problems, anxiety, oversensitivity, and distraction. Sean decided to address emotional healing after noticing the negative impact on his wife and children. He used to drink a lot to calm his nerves, but his doctor said this would make his sleep quality even worse. Sean's kids also said they were afraid of him when he drank.

Sean decided to examine his emotional needs with the following exercise, so he could find healthier solutions.

Examine Your Emotional Needs

Take a deep cleansing breath before reading each question. Then write your responses in the space provided under Sean's examples:

1. What types of validation, understanding, or recognition do you wish you could receive? (Sean's response: "I wish my family would notice how much effort I put into being a good parent. I wanted someone to stop the racist bullying when I was a kid. I wanted the military to stop harassment in ranks. I want recognition at the office for putting in extra work. I wish people would understand I still grieve my dad.")

    _____

    _____

    _____

    _____

2. What sort of blessing do you long for that could be bestowed upon you? (Sean's response: "I wish my supervisor and family would approve of my taking time for getting better. I want the peace of relaxing and sleeping better. I wish that my dad is proud of adult me. I want to feel safe in my body.")

    _____

    _____

    _____

    _____

3. What areas of life do you hope for permission to have? (Sean's response: "I am waiting for someone to give me permission to take time off or do something for the PTSD. I wish I felt permission to talk about my dad.")

_____

_____

_____

_____

4. Do you feel like there are places or people who do provide you with validation, blessing, permission, or recognition? (Sean's response: "My wife plans our family outings and is affectionate and loving. I have colleagues at work who recognize my skills, and my friend Lou listens to me vent.")

_____

_____

_____

_____

5. If you do not receive sufficient validation, blessing, permission, or recognition, what are some ways to seek or create these? (Sean's response: "I can advocate for myself at work and for my health. Writing this down, I realize I have not tried asking for the recognition I want, like I want people to read my mind. I will give myself permission to try out some of the PTSD treatment stuff I have avoided making time for.")

_____

_____

_____

_____

Take a moment to read over your responses. You might even want to reflect and write out your thoughts to these questions when you are in different moods, or to revisit them at another time and see if and how your responses shift. You will likely find some changes in your priorities over time. You may also find that some themes and values always stay true.

Sean found that people were often receptive when he clearly self-advocated for his preferences and needs. His traumas and grief had previously caused him to engage with the world in a defensive and vigilant manner. The more he sought to restore balance, the better understood and seen he felt. Sean allowed himself curiosity to explore and try some therapy options the VA hospital offered such as cognitive behavioral therapy and yoga. Adding trauma-focused yoga and mindfulness skills into this coping toolbox helped Sean reduce his alcohol use and improve his sleep.

Applying Boundaries with Tenacity

You will need to exercise tenacity to pursue your long-term values and goals, pivoting and evolving as needed. Tenacity means showing determination and persistence despite inevitable setbacks, distractions, or even assaults. A research report titled "Academic Tenacity, Mindsets and Skills That Promote Long Term Learning," sponsored by the Bill and Melinda Gates Foundation, highlighted the importance of factors like purpose, belonging, and self-regulation in developing a mindset for perseverance in learning (Dweck, Walton, and Cohen 2014). These are all topics we have explored in this book. Persisting to heal and to seek truth is also a form of tenacity. Your journey using this workbook, creating time to prioritize your healing, is in service of a drive to reclaim the peace and contentment you deserve. Adapting survival skills is a creative and powerful way to protect yourself. Now your efforts are to move beyond survival and toward flourishing.

Figuring out healthy boundaries can be complex. You can expect to receive pushback or an unhappy reaction when you assert yourself in certain situations. For example, you may anticipate an unhappy or even a surprised reaction when you fight back against an unfair situation. On the other hand, sometimes you may be disappointed at receiving a negative reaction from people who ought to be supportive of your well-being and empowerment. Often this comes from community or family members who claim they want what's best for you but won't allow you to assert that choice on your own.

It is often disconcerting for family members when roles and expectations shift. A responsible and healthy parent or caregiver must teach rules, maintain safety, and "be the bad guy," even if their child gets frustrated. As an adult seeking self-determination, you may now find yourself in conflict with your elders or others. You may notice that some people can adjust with time, but others double down and become more rigid. Young adults often notice that their choices are met with anger and resistance. It is important to know when a decision is best in the long term even when someone may be angry at you in the short term. Now you may have to "be the bad guy" and frustrate your elders as you establish safe boundaries and make empowered choices.

Asserting your boundaries can be challenging, as you can see from the following examples of Rami and Melur. Each made empowered choices while receiving pushback from their families.

Indian American Rami's parents were furious when Rami accepted a job in another city. *Rami has an excellent opportunity to direct a team at the new job location, but his parents expected all their adult children to live and settle nearby. Rami's mom is blaming his white fiancé for "brainwashing him," and his father has been screaming at Rami. Rami is grateful to his parents but, for his own mental health, needs some distance from the emotionally abusive climate at home. He doesn't want to argue and is committed to stay firm on his decision.*

Malaysian American Melur is a college student who lives at home with extended family. *This includes her parents, maternal grandmother, and three brothers. When her eldest brother, Enzo, developed a prescription drug problem while in treatment for a back injury, Melur and her family were brokenhearted and terrified to see the impact of drugs. Melur initially reacted to Enzo's scary moods by berating herself, crying for days, and ruminating over all the things she should have done to not upset him. She blamed herself for his behavior. She felt like her family wanted her to appease and "fix" Enzo. In therapy, she rehearsed ways to preserve her mental health while still maintaining values of faith and family. In her prayers, she now wishes Enzo peace, strength, and enlightenment, but has learned to accept she cannot control or be responsible for his emotions and actions. She was able to connect Enzo to Millati Islami, a twelve-step recovery program founded with Islamic principles. People there are kind and nonjudgmental. She is now a volunteer mentor with a youth group at her mosque, which is restoring her sense of purpose.*

You can heighten and build tenacity as you face pushback by surfing the initial waves of emotion and then using your wise mind to examine the situation. Explore options that don't compromise your core values. Acknowledge which aspects are within your control and which are not.

Decide When to Set Boundaries

The next time someone makes a request, and you feel unsure about your boundaries or are wavering in determination, slow down and review your situation. Review the following list of reasons for setting a boundary, and check off any that apply. Then write about the request being made and how you will choose to respond to support your empowerment in this area.

To permit myself to rest without guilt: _____

_____

To ensure safety: _____

_____

To foster personal growth: _____

_____

To stay true to my values: _____

_____

To shift negative generational habits or cycles: _____

_____

To have joy: _____

_____

To avoid resentment: _____

_____

To experience contentment or peace: _____

_____

To be authentic and sincere: _____

_____

To set a good example: _____

_____

To help, not enable others: _____

_____

To avoid burnout: _____

_____

You can download copies of this checklist for future use at http://www.newharbinger.com/52724 to help you decide when to set boundaries.

When Rami completed this exercise, it clarified that if he acceded to his parents' wishes, it would not shift negative generational habits, would make him feel resentful, would not ensure safety, and would fail to foster personal growth and joy. When Melur completed the exercise, she saw that her previous reactions had enabled rather than helped Enzo and had left her feeling exhausted. Her current choices allow her to stay true to her values, be helpful, and be authentic.

Rami and Melur's stories show the importance of asserting interpersonal boundaries. Throughout this workbook you've learned various skills that will help you in asserting healthy boundaries. These begin with the basics of listening to your gut and heart to sense when something is imposing on you in an unconstructive way and then identifying your values and priorities. Boundary-setting skills are about survivance, resilience, and empowering steps toward health.

I hope you will feel improved clarity as you reflect upon your own responses to the key questions of empowerment. Your intuition and sense of values can be a guide to whether the actions, relationships, decisions, or choices you engage with are empowering or disempowering.

Recognize Your Own Tenacity

Give yourself credit for situations in the past when you exerted tenacity in the face of pushback. Perhaps you broke a taboo that was meant to silence you. Perhaps you had to stay firm in the face of someone pressuring you in ways that made you uncomfortable. Then think about how you can use this information now and in the future.

Have you had moments of uncovering the tenacity within yourself? What was the situation?

_____

_____

_____

_____

_____

_____

What are some moments or situations where you would like to exercise more consistent empowerment? How can you stay determined in the face of setbacks or pushback?

_____

_____

_____

_____

_____

_____

_____

Have you admired someone else persisting in defense of their personal or community boundaries? You may have witnessed such determination in a friend or a colleague, or you may have noticed this in a character in a movie. Examples of empowerment and determination can be powerful inspiration. What was the situation?

_____

_____

_____

_____

_____

_____

_____

_____

_____

I want to leave you with a list of some simple ways to assert yourself and voice your limits in any situation. In addition to just saying no, you can say:

Not now.

No thank you.

Not at this time.

I have too many responsibilities.

Sorry I can't help.

I can't handle this, but here are some good resources.

These are all appropriate ways to state your needs. As with starting anything new, ease will come with practice.

This chapter has focused on knowing yourself, developing self-advocacy skills, developing healthy boundaries, and applying the tenacity to consistently protect your values and well-being. Establishing and advocating for your own health is foundational. As you create your story of post-traumatic growth, you will become increasingly defined by what you value and seek. You will need less permission or recognition from others as you strengthen the roots of your own agency. You will find that you are *not* defined by the systems or people that have harmed you. You will more quickly notice when something does not feel right in your gut, as your bodymind intuition guides you. The more aligned your self-talk, thoughts, and actions are with your values and purpose, the more internal peace and flourishing you will uncover. Your journey shall continue long after our time together within these pages. You will continue to write chapters of post-traumatic growth into the story of your life. Thank you for reclaiming space, voice, and health for yourself, for our Asian American communities, for our ancestors, and our future.

We Are
Future
Ancestors

I thank you for allowing me to venture with you into unfamiliar terrain. You are amidst a process of growth, and I am grateful to accompany you on this part of your journey. You may have missed opportunities to be fully cultivated, properly cared for, and lovingly supported. Or you discovered that even the care and love of a family or community cannot prevent every possible danger. Living with the brunt of such challenges and their aftermath does not define you. The baggage and scars of traumas which have haunted your family do not define you. You have always deserved to flourish and experience good things in life. Restoration and recognition of your whole self can take place now, no matter what your age or life stage.

Sometimes you may feel a shadow or feel echoes, triggers of pain. It is my hope that this book has helped you prepare a toolkit of mantras, mindset, rituals, and connections to shield and soothe yourself through the difficult days. Practice both your surfing and your grounding skills to create the flexible responses you need to respond to life's changes. You will coexist with and outpace the past. You will face the ongoing threats and indignities of the world from a center grounded in your values. Embedded beyond grief and rightful anger there are the truths and power of generations of survivance. These are stories of reclaiming fractured selves following devastation. This is your story of post-traumatic growth and reconstruction.

I value your survivance story as courageous, tenacious, and striving toward wholeness. Even if you cannot clearly envision your destination yet, you can move toward restoring wholeness. You cannot know what to expect along the entire journey, but you will proceed forward with each small step in a healthier, more hopeful direction. When you feel stuck, rest a little bit. Then remember that when you don't know what else to do, look to both the past and the future for inspiration. Simultaneously consult ancient wisdom and try something new. Yes, I'm encouraging you to surf that complexity. Try some new course of action, as you have already tried others that led you to getting stuck. New situations can call for new responses. Also consult ancient cultural heritage wisdom, as those practices have been honed for generations to restore bodymind, spirit, and community balance. Adapting some of the old ways will facilitate this journey too.

When you notice you are not flourishing, be curious and examine the sources of concern. Many of life's hindrances are from an entire system, an ecosystem, not just about you. When you purchase a plant from the nursery, it is labeled with a tag that explains the best conditions for this type of plant. The ideal kind of soil, how much sunlight, what temperatures, and how much to fertilize are unique for each plant type. Similarly, you must seek the right combination of environmental conditions and nourishment to flourish personally. On the windowsill of my office, houseplants stretch their leaves and grow toward the sunshine. Please keep stretching yourself toward what is warm and nourishing for you. Understand that like all natural beings, you will have seasons. Some seasons will be warm and cozy, and others may be bitterly cold. Allow yourself the proper care to best move through each season.

The Braitman #writingmedicine workshop, which has been a space for my own healing, has only one rule: no apologies. I want you to hold this in your mind. Sure, you can apologize for mistaken actions, but stop apologizing for being a human being who is processing hard things. Stop apologizing for your tears. Do no apologize for weeping or sobbing, if that is what your heart speaks. Do not apologize for taking up space. No need to apologize for being exhausted. Notice and stay curious about your imperfections, and learn, but you need not apologize. I ask you to notice when you feel the urge to apologize for being human. Instead, notice the feelings, name them, and offer yourself compassion. Speak your authentic truth.

When you have a bad day or a big setback, make time and space to write out your thoughts and to allow your bodymind to express your reactions. We are always a work in progress, developing ourselves and our communities. Use your emotional toolkit and review your emotional trophy case or altar. Speak and write your affirmations. Accept and share social support.

I am honored to be a step in your healing processes. Please continue to seek additional guides, healers, and community spaces. Guides may be licensed mental health professionals, or they may be a martial arts instructor, a cook, a friend, another survivor, a forest, an ancestor, an artist, a teacher, a book, a dog, a bird, a poem, or a song.

Just as you must keep moving your body, you must keep being intentional with your thoughts and mind to maintain the gains and growth you have made. Flex, stretch, and strengthen your mindset along with your physical being. I invite you to periodically revisit this workbook. Your responses to prompts will evolve over time.

There are people across this world who are motivated, like you, to dismantle intergenerational trauma and oppressive systems. Others like you who are externalizing harmful narratives and building shields against manipulation and refusing to participate in colonial mindsets and systemic oppressions. Traumatic experiences can lead you to feel fractured, confused, and untrustful of yourself. I hope these pages have helped you create the spaces and practices to return to your intuition. To be proud of your unique presence in this world. To know that we need you, you belong here, and you can learn to trust yourself again.

I truly hope you receive support, approval, blessings, and permission at each step and juncture ahead. If these are offered to you, accept with both hands. Accept graciously. Gratitude itself is a beautiful healing force. There is no sense in waiting to hit rock bottom before accepting help and support. Use your lifelong learning mindset to continue to add skills and support to your coping toolkit. Why force yourself to do things the hard way when aid and care are present? Our cultural stoicism should not be taken to an extreme that creates hardship. And if no one offers these heart gifts of acceptance to you, I hope you seek environments, guides, and community that can truly see and support you. Cultivating love for yourself makes it easier for others to see and love you. Having love for other beings makes it easier for others to give love in return. Goodwill, empathy, love: these are exchanges with our community that can regenerate and grow rather than deplete us.

Thank you for entering this community of readers and this generation of healers. Healing is something each one of us can foster in ourselves and nurture in the communities all around us. You have the capacity and ability to heal, to pivot, to regenerate, and to ease the trauma of others alongside your own. We are future ancestors. The investments, compassion, and care you extend to yourself is likewise a gift to our communities and future generations.

Filipino families pack a *pabaon* for someone before they depart, a bundle of provisions for the journey. In my family, we also send you off with sustenance. I see you off now with the words, learning, and community stories of these pages. I wrote a scaffold, an outline. The significant parts are customized and to be filled in by your hand. In my heart, I also packed dumplings, cut fruit, and a thermos of Taiwan oolong tea for the next steps of your journey.

I wish you a safe peaceful journey. 一路平安

May you release your fears.

May you flex away stiffness and rigidity.

May you always hold in your mind that healing is possible.

May you replace anxiety with curiosity.

May you allow yourself to rest.

May you feel held and know you are a part of a community of wounded healers.

May you cultivate your humor and energy to balance the burdens and pains.

May you liberate your heart from the burdens and sickness of oppressive systems.

May you liberate your mind from those who have obscured the truth.

May you always walk accompanied by relatives, be they familial or chosen.

May you know the shelter and provision of mutual care.

May your bodymind be nourished always.

May you know and trust your whole self.

Acknowledgments

The creation of a non-academic guidebook for Asian Americans has been something I contemplated for more than a decade. I finally began writing while sequestered in 2020, as worldwide pre-vaccine death tolls mounted. I wrote during a 14-day mandatory COVID quarantine in Taipei, my birthplace. In the midst of that painful season, my scattered mind focused on manifesting a modest contribution to community healing.

My deepest respect and gratitude for the clients, the families, and the communities I have served these past 23 years. It is the greatest honor of my life to be entrusted with your stories and battles, your courage, tenderness, and strength. I hope on some level you have felt in your bones all these years that someone was still wishing you peace and wellness, still rooting for you long after we had parted ways.

All that I have and do comes from the nurturance, principled values, persistence, and joys my family has channeled to me. I am thankful for the resonances of my ancestors, whose survivance through wars, displacement, immigration, racism, and misogyny continues to thrive. All my work has been fueled with mountain oolong tea from Taiwan, and Peet's Coffee, both of which contain a lifetime of shared memories with my dad, Adam Chi Hsu. All my passions were cultivated by the ray of indomitable sunshine that is my mom, Linda Yang Ker-Ming. Mom and Dad, it's been a bumpy road, and I am humbled by your adaptations and sacrifice. Even in the hardest times you gave me priceless books, art, and ethics. Thank you for steadfast love and levity throughout every awkward, inexplicable, tumultuous phase. You guided me to build a voice, a life, and a mission beyond our wildest dreams. My extended family Hsu, Pei, Yang, Leelaluckanakul, Navarro, Tran, Cardamone, and Ong: we've made connections that encompass the world, true generational wealth. Thank you for the years of sustenance and support.

A thousand thanks to the Hella Feminist sisterhood circle of Drs. Katherine Eng, Susan Ono, Kayoko Yokoyama, Sherry Wang, Mina Nguyen, Heather Coleman, Ramani Durvasula, and Michi Fu. Thank you to my Sister Warrior Presidents Drs. Richelle Concepcion, Nellie Tran, Evie Garcia, Iva Graywolf, and Christine Catipon, and my Brother Presidents Drs. Kevin Nadal, Alvin Alvarez,

Kevin Cokley, and Gordon Nagayama Hall. Thank you to the dozens of mentors, particularly Drs. Connie Louie-Handelman, Reiko Homma True, Derald Wing Sue, Carl Mack, the late Reverend Kensho Furuya, and the late Dr. Tim Lukaszewski. I have been encouraged by and taught with staggering generosity and inspired to join in commitment to justice and liberation.

Pruthipong Leelaluckanakul, I mean every word of those lyrics to "Live Long and Prosper." You are my shelter, my muse, my sole unicorn.

Stanford Counseling & Psychological Services; Asian American Psychological Association; APA Divs. 45 and 35; APA Minority Fellowship Program; CrossFit One World; the Okura Mental Health Leadership Foundation; and my relatives in the Association of Black Psychologists; the National Latinx Psychological Association; the Society of Indian Psychologists; and the Association American Arab, Middle Eastern, and North African Psychological Association; and APA Divs. 17 and 44: being in community with you all has been life-sustaining and restorative.

Thank you to Elizabeth Hollis Hansen, Brady Kahn, Jennifer Holder, and New Harbinger for guiding this newbie author with biblical patience. I became a New Harbinger reader 25 years ago during graduate school—it's a wonder to join New Harbinger authors.

Thank you gentle reader for making the time to prioritize you, recognize what you deserve, and include me on this leg of your journey. I look forward to learning from your next chapters.

Resources

Books

Homecoming: Overcome Fear and Trauma to Reclaim Your Whole Authentic Self by Dr. Thema Bryant

Adult Children of Emotionally Immature Parents: How to Heal from Distant, Rejecting, or Self-Involved Parents by Dr. Lindsay C. Gibson

Permission to Come Home: Reclaiming Mental Health as Asian Americans by Dr. Jenny Wang

My Grandmother's Hands: Racialized Trauma and the Pathway to Mending Our Hearts and Bodies by Resmaa Menakem, MSW, LICSW

What My Bones Know: A Memoir About Healing from Complex Trauma by Stephanie Foo

They Called Us Exceptional and Other Lies That Raised Us by Prachi Gupta

Minor Feelings: An Asian American Reckoning by Cathy Park Hong

Filipino American Psychology: A Collection of Personal Narratives by Dr. Kevin L. Nadal

The Pain We Carry: Healing from Complex PTSD for People of Color by Natalie Y. Gutiérrez, LMFT

The Racial Healing Handbook: Practical Activities to Help You Challenge Privilege, Confront Systemic Racism, and Engage in Collective Healing by Dr. Anneliese A. Singh

Racial Melancholia, Racial Dissociation: On the Social and Psychic Lives of Asian Americans by David L. Eng and Shinhee Han

A Wellness Activity Book for Asian Americans by The University of Connecticut's Asian and Asian American Studies Institute, #IAMNOTAVIRUS campaign, and Asian American Literary Review

Break the Cycle: A Guide to Healing Intergenerational Trauma by Dr. Mariel Buqué

Where I Belong: Healing Trauma and Embracing Asian American Identity by Soo Jin Lee and Linda Yoon

What Happened to You? Conversations on Trauma, Resilience, and Healing by Bruce D. Perry and Oprah Winfrey

The Deepest Well: Healing the Long-Term Effects of Childhood Trauma and Adversity by Nadine Burke Harris

Empathy: Why It Matters, and How to Get It by Roman Krznaric

The Mindful Self-Compassion Workbook: A Proven Way to Accept Yourself, Build Inner Strength, and Thrive by Kristin Neff and Christopher Germer

Emotional Intelligence: Why It Can Matter More Than IQ by Daniel Goleman

Crisis Hotlines

988 Suicide Crisis and Hotline. Dial 988 in the United States twenty-four hours a day, seven days a week.

National Sexual Assault Hotline. Confidential support for survivors of sexual abuse and assault, of any and all genders; available twenty-four hours a day, seven days a week at (800) 656-4673.

Trans Lifeline. https://translifeline.org. A peer support service by and for trans people. Confidential and private. No nonconsensual active rescue. Available twenty-four hours a day, seven days a week. In the United States, call (877) 565-8869; Canada (877) 330-6366.

The Trevor Project. Confidential support for LGBTQ+ young people. Available twenty-four hours a day, seven days a week at (866) 488-7386.

Peer and Community Support

National Alliance on Mental Illness (NAMI) information and referral helpline, family to family education: (800) 950-6264

Mental Health Association for Chinese Community (MHACC): https://www.mhacc-usa.org

Asian American Mental Health Collective: https://www.asianmhc.org

Korean American Behavioral Health Association (KABHA): https://www.kabhany.com

Southeast Asian Resource Action Center (SEARAC): https://www.searac.org

Lotus Project: https://www.lotusprojectphi.org

Therapist Directories

Asian American and Native Hawaiian/Pacific Islander Ohana Center of Excellence: https://aanhpi-ohana.org

Asian American Psychological Association: https://www.aapaonline.org

Asian Mental Health Collective: https://www.asianmhc.org

National Deaf Therapy: https://nationaldeaftherapy.com

National Queer Asian Pacific Islander Alliance: https://www.nqapia.org

Substance Abuse and Mental Health Administration referral and information. SAMHSA's National Helpline: 1-800-662-HELP (4357) | 1-800-487-4889 (TTY)

South Asian Therapists: https://www.southasiantherapists.org

YouTube Videos

Asian Mental Health Collective: https://www.youtube.com/@AsianMentalHealthCollective

Dr. Ali Mattu: https://www.youtube.com/c/thepsychshow

Hella Mental Health: https://www.youtube.com/@HellaMentalHealth

Dr. Ramani: https://www.youtube.com/@DoctorRamani

Asian American Psychological Association (AAPA): https://www.youtube.com/@asianamerican
psychological5916/videos

Yellow Chair Collective: https://www.youtube.com/@yellowchaircollective

Apps

Insomnia Coach

PTSD Coach

PTSD Family Coach

ACT Coach

Mindfulness Coach

Breathe2Relax

NextSelf

Mindset by DIVE studios

Podcasts

Asians Do Therapy

Brown Taboo Project

Erasing Shame

Hmong Mental Health

MannMukti Mental Health Podcast

Mental Health Mukbang

References

Ahmed A., S. Mohammed, and D. R. Williams. 2007. "Racial Discrimination and Health: Pathways and Evidence." *Indian Journal of Medical Research* 126(4): 318–327.

Balsam, K. F., Y. Molina, B. Beadnell, J. Simoni, and K. Walters. 2011. "Measuring Multiple Minority Stress: The LGBT People of Color Microaggressions Scale." *Cultural Diversity and Ethnic Minority Psychology* 17(2): 163–174.

Blackwell, K. 2023. "What Does It Mean to Decolonize Your Body?" *New Harbinger* (blog), March 8. https://www.newharbinger.com/blog/self-help/what-does-it-mean-to-decolonize-your-body.

Chin, F., and J. P. Chan. 1972. "Racist Love." In *Seeing Through Shuck*, edited by R. Kostelanetz. New York: Ballantine Books.

Comas-Díaz, L. 2016. "Racial Trauma Recovery: A Race-Informed Therapeutic Approach to Racial Wounds." In *The Cost of Racism for People of Color: Contextualizing Experiences of Discrimination*, edited by A. N. Alvarez, C. T. H. Liang, and H. A. Neville. Washington, DC: American Psychological Association.

Crandall, A. A., J. R. Miller, A. Cheung, L. K. Novilla, R. Glade, M. L. B. Novilla, B. M. Magnusson, B. L. Leavitt, M. D. Barnes, and C. L. Hanson. 2019. "ACEs and Counter-ACEs: How Positive and Negative Childhood Experiences Influence Adult Health." *Child Abuse and Neglect* 96: 104089.

Dixon, M. L., and C. S. Dweck. 2022. "The Amygdala and the Prefrontal Cortex: The Co-Construction of Intelligent Decision-Making." *Psychological Review* 129(6): 1414–1441.

Dweck, C. S., G. M. Walton, and G. L. Cohen. 2014. *Academic Tenacity: Mindsets and Skills That Promote Long-Term Learning.* Seattle: Bill and Melinda Gates Foundation. https://ed.stanford.edu/sites/default/files/manual/dweck-walton-cohen-2014.pdf.

Furuyashiki, A., K. Tabuchi, K. Norikoshi, T. Kobayashi, and S. Oriyama. 2019. "A Comparative Study of the Physiological and Psychological Effects of Forest Bathing (Shinrin-Yoku) on

Working Age People with and Without Depressive Tendencies." *Environmental Health and Preventative Medicine* 24: 46.

Goleman, D. 1995. *Emotional Intelligence: Why It Can Matter More Than IQ.* New York: Bantam Books.

Gupta, P. 2023. *They Called Us Exceptional, and Other Lies That Raised Us.* New York: Crown.

Hall, G. C. N., E. T. Berkman, N. W. Zane, F. T. L. Leong, W.-C. Hwang, A. M. Nezu, C. M. Nezu, J. J. Hong, J. P. Chu, and E. R. Huang. 2021. "Reducing Mental Health Disparities by Increasing the Personal Relevance of Interventions." *American Psychologist* 76(1): 91–103.

Linehan, M. M. 2014. *DBT Skills Training Manual,* 2nd ed. New York: Guilford Press.

Mosley, D. V., H. A. Neville, N. Y. Chavez-Dueñas, H. Y. Adames, J. A. Lewis, and B. H. French. 2020. "Radical Hope in Revolting Times: Proposing a Culturally Relevant Psychological Framework." *Social and Personality Psychology Compass* 14(1): e12512.

Nadal, K. L. 2012. *Filipino American Psychology: A Handbook of Theory, Research, and Clinical Practice.* Hoboken, NJ: John Wiley & Sons.

Neville, H. 2021. "Radical Healing: Psychological Interventions with Black, Indigenous, and People of Color." Paper presented at The Evolution of Psychotherapy, virtual conference, December 1–5.

Nhat Hanh, T. 2014. *No Mud, No Lotus: The Art of Transforming Suffering.* Berkeley, CA: Parallax Press.

Office of the US Surgeon General. 2023. *Our Epidemic of Loneliness and Isolation: The US Surgeon General's Advisory on the Healing Effects of Social Connection and Community.* Washington, DC. https://www.hhs.gov/sites/default/files/surgeon-general-social-connection-advisory.pdf.

Parker, K., J. Horowitz, A. Brown, R. Fry, D. Cohn, and R. Igielnik. 2018. "What Unites and Divides Urban, Suburban, and Rural Communities." Pew Research Center, May 22. https://www.pewresearch.org/social-trends/2018/05/22/what-unites-and-divides-urban-suburban-and-rural-communities.

Rogol, A. D. 2020. "Emotional Deprivation in Children: Growth Faltering and *Reversible* Hypopituitarism." *Frontiers in Endocrinology* 11: 596144.

Sandstrom, G. M., and E. W. Dunn. 2014. "Social Interactions and Well-Being: The Surprising Power of Weak Ties." *Personality and Social Psychology Bulletin* 40(7): 910–922.

Sapolsky, R. M. 2004. *Why Zebras Don't Get Ulcers: The Acclaimed Guide to Stress, Stress-Related Diseases, and Coping*, 3rd ed. New York: Holt.

Shao, D. 2023. "Is There a Bamboo Ceiling? The Asian-White Gap in Managerial Attainment for College-Educated Workers." *Sociology of Race and Ethnicity* 9(1): 87–102.

Siagatonu, T. 2023. "What's Good, Fam? I'm Terisa." https://www.terisasiagatonu.com.

Sleeter, C. E., and M. Zavala. 2020. *Transformative Ethnic Studies in Schools: Curriculum, Pedagogy, and Research*. New York: Teachers College Press.

Steiner, J. G. Sheremenko, C. Lesesne, P. J. Dittus, R. E. Sieving, and K. A. Ethier. 2019. "Adolescent Connectedness and Adult Health Outcomes." *Pediatrics* 144(1): e20183766.

Stephens, M. J. 2021. "2020: The Year We Lost Our Breath." *Each Breath by the American Lung Association* (blog), March 29. https://www.lung.org/blog/2020-breath.

Sue, D. W., and D. Sue. 1990. *Counseling the Culturally Different: Theory and Practice*, 2nd ed. New York: John Wiley & Sons.

Ulrich, R. S. 1984. "View Through a Window May Influence Recovery from Surgery." *Science* 224(4647): 420–421.

VanderWeele, T. J. 2017. "On the Promotion of Human Flourishing." *Proceedings of the National Academy of Science of the United States of America* 114(31): 8148–8156.

Zaki, J. 2019. *The War for Kindness: Building Empathy in a Fractured World*. New York: Broadway Books.

Zheng, L., and I. Hansen. 2019. *The Ethical Sell Out: Maintaining Your Integrity in the Age of Compromise*. Oakland, CA: Berrett-Koehler Publishers.

Helen H. Hsu, PsyD, is a licensed clinical psychologist at Stanford University. She is past president of the Asian American Psychological Association and the American Psychological Association, Division 45: Society for the Psychological Study of Culture, Ethnicity, and Race. She lives in the San Francisco Bay Area.

Foreword writer **Ali Mattu, PhD**, is a clinical psychologist who has spent a decade treating anxiety disorders. He has shifted his focus to public education in order to create more scalable forms of mental health support. You can see his work at www.youtube.com/@drali.

Real change *is* possible

For more than forty-five years, New Harbinger has published proven-effective self-help books and pioneering workbooks to help readers of all ages and backgrounds improve mental health and well-being, and achieve lasting personal growth. In addition, our spirituality books offer profound guidance for deepening awareness and cultivating healing, self-discovery, and fulfillment.

Founded by psychologist Matthew McKay and Patrick Fanning, New Harbinger is proud to be an independent, employee-owned company. Our books reflect our core values of integrity, innovation, commitment, sustainability, compassion, and trust. Written by leaders in the field and recommended by therapists worldwide, New Harbinger books are practical, accessible, and provide real tools for real change.

MORE BOOKS from
NEW HARBINGER PUBLICATIONS

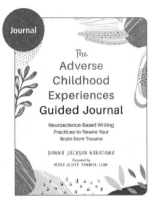
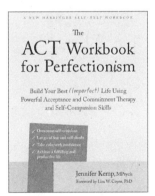

Did you know there are **free tools** you can download for this book?

Free tools are things like **worksheets**, **guided meditation exercises**, and **more** that will help you get the most out of your book.

You can download free tools for this book— whether you bought or borrowed it, in any format, from any source—from the New Harbinger website. All you need is a NewHarbinger.com account. Just use the URL provided in this book to view the free tools that are available for it. Then, click on the "download" button for the free tool you want, and follow the prompts that appear to log in to your NewHarbinger.com account and download the material.

You can also save the free tools for this book to your **Free Tools Library** so you can access them again anytime, just by logging in to your account! Just look for this button on the book's free tools page.

+ Save this to my free tools library

If you need help accessing or downloading free tools, visit **newharbinger.com/faq** or contact us at **customerservice@newharbinger.com**.